... I went to the angel and told him to give me the little scroll; and he said to me, "Take it and eat; it will be bitter in your stomach, but sweet as honey in your mouth." And I took the little scroll from the hand of the angel and ate it; it was sweet as honey in my mouth, but when I had eaten it my stomach was made bitter.

ST. JOHN THE THEOLOGIAN

Eat This Book

A CONVERSATION IN THE ART
OF SPIRITUAL READING

Eugene H. Peterson

Hodder & Stoughton
LONDON SYDNEY AUCKLAND

First published in Great Britain in 2006,
by arrangement with Wm. Eerdmans Publishing Co.
Published in association with the literary agency of
Alive Communications, Inc.,
7680 Goddard Street #200, Colorado Springs, CO 80290

2

British Library Cataloguing in Publication Data
A record for this book is available from the British Library

ISBN 0 340 86391 9

Printed and bound in Great Britain by
Clays Ltd, St Ives plc

The paper and board used in this paperback are natural recyclable products made from
wood grown in sustainable forests. The manufacturing processes conform to the
environmental regulations of the country of origin.

Hodder & Stoughton
A Division of Hodder Headline Ltd
338 Euston Road
London NW1 3BH
www.madaboutbooks.com
and
www.hodderbibles.co.uk

For Jon and Cheryl Stine

faithful companions in the vineyard of the text

Contents

Acknowledgments

Early drafts of this material, now considerably revised, appeared in the journals *Crux* and *Theology Today*. Portions of the manuscript were given as lectures at Regent College, Vancouver, as the Glenhoe Lectures at Louisville Seminary, and at the Schloss-Mittersill Study Center, Switzerland. Some of the material on metaphor in chapter seven comes from *Where Your Treasure Is* (Eerdmans, 1993).

Professor Iain Provain and Professor Sven Soderlund, colleagues at Regent College, gave a careful reading to the manuscript. Their help has been invaluable, improving the material beyond what I was capable of by myself. Jon and Cheryl Stine have been sturdy and continuing companions in the unending task of preparing meals in which the main course is the word of God; *Eat This Book* is dedicated to them.

Preface

My wife picked up our seven-year-old grandson at noon on an October Saturday at Holy Nativity Church. Hans had been attending a class in preparation for his First Communion. They drove off, headed to a local museum that was featuring a special children's exhibit on gemstones. On the way they stopped at a city park to eat their lunches. The two of them ate while sitting on a park bench, Hans chattering all the while — he had been chattering nonstop ever since leaving the church. Lunch completed — his was a lettuce and mayonnaise sandwich that he had made himself ("I'm trying to eat more healthy, Grandma") — Hans shifted away from his grandmother, faced out into the park, took from his bookbag a New Testament that he had just been given by his pastor, opened it, held it up before his eyes, and proceeded to read, moving his eyes back and forth across the page in a devout but uncharacteristic silence. After a long minute, he closed the Testament and returned it to his bookbag; "Okay, Grandma, I'm ready — let's go to the museum."

His grandmother was impressed. She was also amused because Hans cannot yet read. He wants to read. His sister can read. Some of his friends can read. But Hans can't read. And he *knows* he can't read, sometimes announcing to us, "I can't read," as if to reinforce our awareness of what he is missing.

So what was he doing, "reading" his New Testament on the park bench that autumn Saturday?

When my wife later told me the story, I also was impressed and amused. But after a few days the story developed in my imagination into a parable. At the time I was immersed in writing this book, an extended conversation in the practice of spiritual reading; I was finding it hard to keep my hoped-for readers in focus. They kept blurring into a faceless crowd of Bible-readers and Bible-nonreaders, Bible teachers and Bible preachers. Is there an impediment, a difficulty, that we all share in common when we pick up our Bibles and open them? I think there is. Hans gave me my focus.

*   *   *

I have been at this business of reading the Bible ever since I was not much older than Hans. Twenty years after I first started reading it I became a pastor and a professor; for over fifty years now I have been vocationally involved in getting the Christian Scriptures into the minds and hearts, arms and legs, ears and mouths of men and women. And I haven't found it easy. Why isn't it easy?

Simply this. The challenge — never negligible — regarding the Christian Scriptures is getting them read, but read on their own terms, as God's revelation. It seems as if it would be the easiest thing in the world. After five or six years of schooling, schooling that the whole community pitches in to pay for, most of us can read most of what is written in the Bible. If you don't own one and can't afford to buy one, you can steal a Bible from nearly any hotel or motel in the country. And without fear of arrest — who has ever been arrested on a misdemeanor charge for stealing a Bible in this fair land?

But as it turns out, in this business of living the Christian life, ranking high among the most neglected aspects is one having to do with the reading of the Christian Scriptures. Not that Christians don't own and read their Bibles. And not that Christians don't believe that their Bibles are the word of God. What is neglected is reading the Scriptures formatively, reading in order to live.

Hans on that park bench, his eyes moving back and forth across the pages of his Bible, "reading" but not reading, reverent and devout but uncomprehending, honoring in a most precious way this book but without awareness that it has anything to do with either the lettuce and mayonnaise sandwich he has just eaten or the museum he is about to visit, oblivious to his grandmother next to him: Hans "reading" his Bible. A parable.

A parable of the Scriptures depersonalized into an object to be honored; the Scriptures detached from precedence and consequence, from lunch and museum; the Scriptures in a park elevated over life on the street, a book-on-a-pedestal text, buffered by an expansive and manicured lawn from the noise and stink of diesel-fueled eighteen-wheelers.

It is the devil's own work to take what is presently endearing and innocent in Hans and perpetuate it into a lifetime of reading marked by devout indifference.

What I want to say, countering the devil, is that in order to read the Scriptures adequately and accurately, it is necessary at the same time to live them. Not to live them as a prerequisite to reading them, and not to live them in consequence of reading them, but to live them *as* we read them, the living and reading reciprocal, body language and spoken words, the back-and-forthness assimilating the reading to the living, the living to the reading. Reading the Scriptures is not an activity discrete from living the gospel but one integral to it. It means letting Another have a say in everything we are saying and doing. It is as easy as that. And as hard.

CHAPTER 1

"The Forbidding Discipline of Spiritual Reading"

Years ago I owned a dog who had a fondness for large bones. Fortunately for him we lived in the forested foothills of Montana. In his forest rambles he often came across a carcass of a white-tailed deer that had been brought down by the coyotes. Later he would show up on our stone, lakeside patio carrying or dragging his trophy, usually a shank or a rib; he was a small dog and the bone was often nearly as large as he was. Anyone who has owned a dog knows the routine: he would prance and gambol playfully before us with his prize, wagging his tail, proud of his find, courting our approval. And of course, we approved: we lavished praise, telling him what a good dog he was. But after awhile, sated with our applause, he would drag the bone off twenty yards or so to a more private place, usually the shade of a large moss-covered boulder, and go to work on the bone. The social aspects of the bone were behind him; now the pleasure became solitary. He gnawed the bone, turned it over and around, licked it, worried it. Sometimes we could hear a low rumble or growl, what in a cat would be a purr. He was obviously enjoying himself and in no hurry. After a leisurely couple of hours he would bury it and return the next day to take it up again. An average bone lasted about a week.

I always took delight in my dog's delight, his playful seriousness, his childlike spontaneities now totally absorbed in "the one thing needful." But imagine my further delight in coming upon a phrase one day while reading Isaiah in which I found the poet-prophet observing something similar to what I enjoyed so much in my dog, except that his animal was a lion instead of a dog: "As a lion or a young lion growls over his prey . . ." (Isa. 31:4). "Growls" is the word that caught my attention and brought me that little "pop" of delight. What my dog did over his precious bone, making those low throaty rumbles of pleasure as he gnawed, enjoyed, and savored his prize, Isaiah's lion did to his prey. The nugget of my delight was noticing the Hebrew word here translated as "growl" *(hagah)* but usually translated as "meditate," as in the Psalm 1 phrase describing the blessed man or woman whose "delight is in the law of the LORD," on which "he meditates day and night" (v. 2). Or in Psalm 63: "when I think of thee upon my bed, and meditate on thee in the watches of the night" (v. 6). But Isaiah uses this word to refer to a lion growling over his prey the way my dog worried a bone.

Hagah is a word that our Hebrew ancestors used frequently for reading the kind of writing that deals with our souls. But "meditate" is far too tame a word for what is being signified. "Meditate" seems more suited to what I do in a quiet chapel on my knees with a candle burning on the altar. Or to what my wife does while sitting in a rose garden with the Bible open in her lap. But when Isaiah's lion and my dog meditated they chewed and swallowed, using teeth and tongue, stomach and intestines: Isaiah's lion meditating his goat (if that's what it was); my dog meditating his bone. There is a certain kind of writing that invites this kind of reading, soft purrs and low growls as we taste and savor, anticipate and take in the sweet and spicy, mouth-watering and soul-energizing morsel words — "O taste and see that the LORD is good!" (Ps. 34:8). Isaiah uses the same word *(hagah)* a few pages later for the cooing of a dove (38:14). One careful reader of this text caught the spirit of the word when he said that *hagah* means that a person "is lost in his religion,"[1] which is exactly what my dog was in his bone. Baron Friedrich von Hügel compared this way of reading to

---

1. A. Negoita, *Theological Dictionary of the Old Testament*, ed. G. Johannes Botterweck and Helmer Ringgren (Grand Rapids: Eerdmans, 1978), vol. 3, p. 321.

"letting a very slowly dissolving lozenge melt imperceptibly in your mouth."[2]

*   *   *

I am interested in cultivating this kind of reading, the only kind of reading that is congruent with what is written in our Holy Scriptures, but also with all writing that is intended to change our lives and not just stuff some information into the cells of our brain. All serious and good writing anticipates precisely this kind of reading — ruminative and leisurely, a dalliance with words in contrast to wolfing down information. But our canonical writers who wrestled God's revelation into Hebrew, Aramaic, and Greek sentences — Moses and Isaiah, Ezekiel and Jeremiah, Mark and Paul, Luke and John, Matthew and David, along with their numerous brothers and sisters, named and unnamed across the centuries — absolutely require it. They make up a school of writers employed by the Holy Spirit to give us our Holy Scriptures and keep us in touch with and responsive to reality, whether visible or invisible: God-reality, God-presence. They are all distinguished by a deep trust in the "power of words" (Coleridge's phrase) to bring us into the presence of God and to change our lives. By keeping company with the writers of Holy Scripture we are schooled in a practice of reading and writing that is infused with an enormous respect — more than respect, awed reverence — for the revelatory and transformative power of words. The opening page of the Christian text for living, the Bible, tells us that the entire cosmos and every living creature in it are brought into being by words. St. John selects the term "Word" to account, first and last, for what is most characteristic about Jesus, the person at the revealed and revealing center of the Christian story. Language, spoken and written, is the primary means for getting us in on what *is*, on what God is and is doing. But it is language of a certain stripe, not words external to our lives, the sort used in grocery lists, computer manuals, French grammars, and basketball rulebooks.

2. Baron Friedrich von Hügel, *Selected Letters* (New York: E. P. Dutton, 1927), p. 229.

These are words intended, whether confrontationally or obliquely, to get inside us, to deal with our souls, to form a life that is congruent with the world that God has created, the salvation that he has enacted, and the community that he has gathered. Such writing anticipates and counts on a certain kind of reading, a dog-with-a-bone kind of reading.

Writers of other faith traditions and writers who hold to none — atheists, agnostics, secularists — also, of course, have access to this school and benefit enormously from its training in the holiness of words. But the adjective "spiritual" does serve to identify the way the writers who collectively scribed the Bible used language to form "the mind of Christ" in their readers. The adjective continues to be useful in identifying the post-biblical men and women who continue to write journalism and commentary, studies and reflections, stories and poems for us as we continue to submit our imaginations to the shaping syntax and diction of our biblical masters. But Holy Scripture is the source document, the authoritative font, the work of the Spirit that is definitive in all true spirituality.

What I mean to insist upon is that spiritual writing — *Spirit-sourced writing* — requires spiritual reading, a reading that honors words as holy, words as a basic means of forming an intricate web of relationships between God and the human, between all things visible and invisible.

There is only one way of reading that is congruent with our Holy Scriptures, writing that trusts in the power of words to penetrate our lives and create truth and beauty and goodness, writing that requires a reader who, in the words of Rainer Maria Rilke, "does not always remain bent over his pages; he often leans back and closes his eyes over a line he has been reading again, and its meaning spreads through his blood."[3] This is the kind of reading named by our ancestors as *lectio divina*, often translated "spiritual reading," reading that enters our souls as food enters our stomachs, spreads through our blood, and becomes holiness and love and wisdom.

---

3. Rainer Maria Rilke, *The Notebooks of Malte Laurids Brigge*, trans. M. D. Herter (New York: W. W. Norton, 1954), p. 201.

*　　*　　*

In 1916 a young Swiss pastor, Karl Barth, gave an address in the neighboring village of Leutwil where his friend Eduard Thurneysen was pastor. Barth was thirty years old, had been a pastor in Safenwil for five years, and was just beginning to discover the Bible. A few miles away the rest of Europe was on fire with war, a war epidemic with lies and carnage that marked what one writer at the time (Karl Kraus) called the "irreparable termination of what was humane in Western civilization."[4] Each succeeding decade of the century supplied more details — political, cultural, and spiritual evidence of the world inexorably becoming what T. S. Eliot had laid out in prescient poetry as "The Waste Land."

At the time that the killing and lying were in full spate, just across the German and French borders in neutral Switzerland this young pastor had discovered the Bible as if for the first time, discovered it as a book absolutely unique, unprecedented. The soul and body of Europe, and eventually the world, was being violated. On every continent millions were hanging on news from "the front" and on speeches from the world's leaders as reported by the journalists. Meanwhile Barth, in his small out-of-the-way village, was writing what he had discovered, the extraordinary truth-releasing, God-witnessing, culture-challenging realities in this book, the Bible. After a few years he published what he had discovered in his commentary, *Epistle to the Romans*. It was the first in a procession of books that in the years to come would convince many Christians that the Bible was giving a truer, more accurate account of what was going on in their seemingly unraveling world than what their politicians and journalists were telling them. At the same time Barth determined to recover the capacity of Christians to *read* the book receptively in its original, transformative character. Barth brought the Bible out of the academic mothballs in which it had been stored for so long for so many. He demonstrated how presently alive it

4. Quoted in George Steiner, *Grammars of Creation* (New Haven: Yale University Press, 2001), p. 269.

is, and how different it is from books that can be "handled" — dissected and analyzed and then used for whatever we want them for. He showed, clearly and persuasively, that this "different" kind of writing (revelatory and intimate instead of informational and impersonal) must be met by a different kind of reading (receptive and leisurely instead of standoffish and efficient). He also kept calling attention to writers who had absorbed and continued to write in the biblical style, involving us as readers in life-transforming responses. Dostoevsky, for instance, as the Russian reproduced in his novels the radical Genesis reversals of human assessments, shaping his characters under the rubric of the divine "nevertheless" and not as the divine "therefore."

Later Barth published his Leutwil address under the title "The Strange New World within the Bible."[5] At a time and in a culture in which the Bible had been embalmed and buried by a couple of generations of undertaker-scholars, he passionately and relentlessly insisted that "the child is not dead but sleeping," took her by the hand, and said, "Arise." For the next fifty years, Barth demonstrated the incredible vigor and energy radiating from the sentences and stories of this book and showed us how to read them.

*   *   *

Barth insists that we do not read this book and the subsequent writings that are shaped by it in order to find out how to get God into our lives, get him to participate in our lives. No. We open this book and find that page after page it takes us off guard, surprises us, and draws us into *its* reality, pulls us into participation with God on *his* terms.

He provided an illustration that became famous. I am using the germ of his anecdote but furnishing it, with a little help from Walker Percy,[6] with my own details. Imagine a group of men and women in a

5. In Karl Barth, *The Word of God and the Word of Man* (Gloucester, Mass.: Peter Smith, 1978 [first published in 1928]), pp. 28-50.

6. See Walker Percy, *The Message in the Bottle* (New York: Farrar, Straus and Giroux, 1975), pp. 119-49.

huge warehouse. They were born in this warehouse, grew up in it, and have everything there for their needs and comfort. There are no exits to the building but there are windows. But the windows are thick with dust, are never cleaned, and so no one bothers to look out. Why would they? The warehouse is everything they know, has everything they need. But then one day one of the children drags a stepstool under one of the windows, scrapes off the grime, and looks out. He sees people walking on the streets; he calls to his friends to come and look. They crowd around the window — they never knew a world existed outside their warehouse. And then they notice a person out in the street looking up and pointing; soon several people are gathered, looking up and talking excitedly. The children look up but there is nothing to see but the roof of their warehouse. They finally get tired of watching these people out on the street acting crazily, pointing up at nothing and getting excited about it. What's the point of stopping for no reason at all, pointing at nothing at all, and talking up a storm about the nothing?

But what those people in the street were looking at was an airplane (or geese in flight, or a gigantic pile of cumulus clouds). The people in the street look up and see the heavens and everything in the heavens. The warehouse people have no heavens above them, just a roof.

What would happen, though, if one day one of those kids cut a door out of the warehouse, coaxed his friends out, and discovered the immense sky above them and the grand horizons beyond them? That is what happens, writes Barth, when we open the Bible — we enter the totally unfamiliar world of God, a world of creation and salvation stretching endlessly above and beyond us. Life in the warehouse never prepared us for anything like this.

Typically, adults in the warehouse scoff at the tales the children bring back. After all, they are completely in control of the warehouse world in ways they could never be outside. And they want to keep it that way.

*   *   *

St. Paul was the little kid who first scraped the grime off the window for Barth, cut out a door, and coaxed him outdoors into the large, "strange" world to which the biblical writers give witness. Under this school of writers, beginning with St. Paul but soon including the entire Holy Spirit faculty, Barth became a Christian *reader,* reading words in order to be formed by the Word. Only then did he become a Christian *writer.*

Barth's account of what had happened to him was later published in *The Word of God and the Word of Man.* Novelist John Updike said that that book "gave me a philosophy to live and labor by, and in that way changed my life." On receiving the Campion medal in 1997, Updike credited the Christian faith revealed in Barth's rediscovered Bible for telling him, as a writer, "that truth is holy, and truth-telling a noble and useful profession; that the reality around us is created and worth celebrating; that men and women are radically imperfect and radically valuable."[7]

*   *   *

The first metaphors for writing and reading that caught my fancy were from Kafka: "If the book we are reading does not wake us, as with a fist hammering on our skull, why then do we read it? . . . A book must be like an ice-axe to break the frozen sea within us."[8] By this time I was vocationally involved as a pastor and professor in getting people involved in the right reading of Scripture. I was dismayed that their reading of the Bible didn't seem to be any different from the way they read the sports page, or the comic strips, or the want ads. I wanted to wake people up and turn them inside out. I wanted them to see the Bible as a fisticuff book, an ice-axe book. In retrospect I realize that my strategy was mostly carried out by raising my voice. I hardly noticed the violence in the metaphors; I wanted to *make a difference.* And then I was caught up short by Wendell Berry's question: "Did you finish killing / everybody

7. John Updike, *More Matter* (New York: Alfred A. Knopf, 1999), pp. 843, 851.
8. Quoted by George Steiner, *Language and Silence* (New York: Atheneum, 1970), p. 67.

who was against peace?"[9] I realized that the violence implicit in the metaphors wasn't exactly suited to what I had in mind as I was trying to guide Christian readers to receive the words of Holy Scripture as food for their souls. Maybe force-feeding isn't the best way to convey the distinctive quality inherent in Bible reading, in spiritual reading.

And then I noticed that the most striking biblical metaphor for reading was St. John eating a book:

> I went to the angel and told him to give me the little scroll; and he said to me, "Take it, and eat; it will be bitter to your stomach, but sweet as honey in your mouth." And I took the little scroll from the hand of the angel and ate it; it was sweet as honey in my mouth, but when I had eaten it my stomach was made bitter. (Rev. 10:9-10)

Jeremiah and Ezekiel before him had also eaten books — a good diet, it would seem, for anyone who cares about reading words rightly.

For attention-getting, this is as good as Kafka any day, but as metaphor it is far better. St. John, this endlessly fascinating early-church apostle and pastor and writer, walks up to the angel and says, "Give me the book." The angel hands it over, "Here it is; eat it, eat the book." And John does. He eats the book — not *just* reads it — he got it into his nerve endings, his reflexes, his imagination. The book he ate was Holy Scripture. Assimilated into his worship and prayer, his imagining and writing, the book he ate was metabolized into the book he wrote, the first great poem in the Christian tradition and the concluding book of the Bible, the Revelation.

*　　*　　*

The Oxford don Austin Farrer, in his Bampton Lectures, referred to "the forbidding discipline of spiritual reading"[10] that ordinary people

---

9. Wendell Berry, *Collected Poems 1957-1982* (San Francisco: North Point, 1985), p. 121.

10. Austin Farrer, *The Glass of Vision* (Westminster: Dacre, 1948), p. 36.

have characteristically brought to this text that forms their souls. Forbidding because it requires that we read with our entire life, not just employing the synapses in our brain. Forbidding because of the endless dodges we devise in avoiding the risk of faith in God. Forbidding because of our restless inventiveness in using whatever knowledge of "spirituality" we acquire to set ourselves up as gods. Forbidding because when we have learned to read and comprehend the words on the page, we find that we have hardly begun. Forbidding because it requires all of us, our muscles and ligaments, our eyes and ears, our obedience and adoration, our imaginations and our prayers. Our ancestors set this "forbidding discipline" (their phrase for it was *lectio divina*)[11] as the core curriculum in this most demanding of all schools, the School of the Holy Spirit, established by Jesus when he told his disciples, "When the Spirit of truth comes, he will guide you into all the truth . . . he will take what is mine and declare it to you" (John 16:13-15; also 14:16; 15:26; 16:7-8). All writing that comes out of this School anticipates this kind of reading: participatory reading, receiving the words in such a way that they become interior to our lives, the rhythms and images becoming practices of prayer, acts of obedience, ways of love.

Words spoken or written to us under the metaphor of eating, words to be freely taken in, tasted, chewed, savored, swallowed, and digested, have a very different effect on us from those that come at us from the outside, whether in the form of propaganda or information. Propaganda works another person's will upon us, attempting to manipulate us to an action or a belief. Insofar as we are moved by it, we become less, the puppet of a puppeteer writer/speaker. There is no dignity, no soul, in a puppet. And information reduces words to the condition of commodities that we can use however we will. Words are removed from their originating context in the moral universe and from personal relationships so that they can be used as tools or weapons. Such commodification of language reduces both those who speak it and those who listen to it also to commodities.

11. The details involved in this "forbidding" will be elaborated in Section II, *Lectio Divina*.

Reading is an immense gift, but only if the words are assimilated, taken into the soul — eaten, chewed, gnawed, received in unhurried delight. Words of men and women long dead, or separated by miles and/or years, come off the page and enter our lives freshly and precisely, conveying truth and beauty and goodness, words that God's Spirit has used and uses to breathe life into our souls. Our access to reality deepens into past centuries, spreads across continents. But this reading also carries with it subtle dangers. Passionate words of men and women spoken in ecstasy can end up flattened on the page and dissected with an impersonal eye. Wild words wrung out of excruciating suffering can be skinned and stuffed, mounted and labeled as museum specimens. The danger in all reading is that words be twisted into propaganda or reduced to information, mere tools and data. We silence the living voice and reduce words to what we can use for convenience and profit.

One psalmist mocked his contemporaries for reducing the living God who spoke and listened to them into a gold or silver thing-god that they could use:

> Those who make them are like them;
> so are all who trust in them. (Ps. 115:8)

It's an apt warning for us still as we deal daily with the incredible explosion of information technology and propagandizing techniques. These words need rescuing.

I

EAT THIS BOOK

"I am the bread of life. Your ancestors ate the manna in the wilderness, and they died. This is the bread that comes down from heaven, so that one may eat of it and not die."

JOHN 6:48-50 NRSV

"To know much and taste nothing — of what use is that?"

BONAVENTURE

CHAPTER 2

The Holy Community
at Table with Holy Scripture

The Christian Scriptures are the primary text for Christian spirituality. Christian spirituality is, in its entirety, rooted in and shaped by the scriptural text. We don't form our personal spiritual lives out of a random assemblage of favorite texts in combination with individual circumstances; we are formed by the Holy Spirit in accordance with the text of Holy Scripture. God does not put us in charge of forming our personal spiritualities. We grow in accordance with the revealed Word implanted in us by the Spirit.

The commanding presence of Holy Scripture as the formative text for the Christian has never gone unchallenged. Through the centuries people have found that they preferred other ways of going about this business of finding direction and guidance for living the Christian life. But the church community has consistently said "no" to them and kept a firm grip on this text, this authoritative Bible.

We have said "no," for instance, to working ourselves up into visionary states of ecstasy in order to get in touch with God. Heightened emotional states are very attractive, particularly to adolescents. There is such a thrilling sense of immediacy to it; it feels so, well, *authentic*, so *alive*. The generic designation "enthusiasm" has been attached to this way of the soul that has attracted and continues to attract so many off on detours of self-gratification and into addictive cul de sacs. Our wisest teachers have always steered us away from them.[1] We say "no" to undertaking Herculean tasks of moral heroism in order to call up and display the divine potentialities within us. The challenge of heroics, especially moral heroics, pumps adrenalin into our bloodstream and frees us from the neighborhood mediocrities that mire us in the mud of the commonplace. We say "no" to going off to a mountain cave and emptying ourselves of all thought, feeling, and desire so that there is nothing left in us to separate us from immediate access to reality. There is something so pure, so simple, so uncluttered about it. The Zen koan displaces Christian Scripture.

But the "text" that seems to be most in favor on the American landscape today is the sovereign self. A friend told me recently of an acquaintance, a lifelong reader of the Bible, who realized one day that his life was not turning out as he thought the Bible said it would. He decided then and there, in his words, to "make my life my authority instead of the Bible." Most of our culture, both secular and religious, supports the man's decision. It has become characteristic of our burgeoning, contemporary spirituality in its various manifestations to take the sovereign self as text. But the results are not encouraging: the groundswell of interest in spirituality as this new millennium has opened up does not seem to be producing any discernible outpouring of energetic justice and faithful love, two of the more obvious accompaniments of a healthy and holy Christian life. In fact, we have arrived at a point now when the term "spirituality" is more apt to call to mind dabblers in transcendence than lives of rigor, exuberance, goodness, and justice — the kinds of lives historically associated with this word.

Christians can hardly fail to take account of the popularity of these self-sovereign spiritualities, sometimes to be impressed by some of the spiritual pyrotechnics, occasionally even to ooh and aah over them. But mature reflection doesn't provide encouragement to go in for them ourselves. In contrast to the self-serving and glamorous spiritualities, ours is a pedestrian way, literally pedestrian: we put one

1. See Ronald Knox, *Enthusiasm* (New York: Oxford University Press, 1961 [first published in 1950]).

foot in front of the other as we follow Jesus. And in order to know who he is, where he is going, and how to walk in his steps, we reach for a book, *the* book, and read it.

*   *   *

I want to counter this widespread practice of taking personal experience instead of the Bible as the authority for living. I want to pull the Christian Scriptures back from the margins of the contemporary imagination where they have been so rudely elbowed by their glamorous competitors, and reestablish them at the center as the text for living the Christian life deeply and well. I want to confront and expose this replacement of the authoritative Bible by the authoritative self. I want to place personal experience under the authority of the Bible and not over it. I want to set the Bible before us as the text by which we live our lives, this text that stands in such sturdy contrast to the potpourri of religious psychology, self-development, mystical experimentation, and devotional dilettantism that has come to characterize so much of what takes cover under the umbrella of "spirituality."

There is an enormous interest these days in the soul. In the church this interest in the soul is evidenced in a revival of attention in matters of spiritual theology, spiritual leadership, spiritual direction, and spiritual formation. But there is not a corresponding revival of interest in our Holy Scriptures. Spiritual theology, spiritual leadership, spiritual direction, and spiritual formation require that we tend to the work of the Holy Spirit in our individual and corporate, public and political lives. But those who are enthusiastic about this work are frequently, even typically, disinterested in the Holy Scriptures, the book that is given to us by the Holy Spirit. It is a matter of urgency that interest in our souls be matched by an interest in our Scriptures — and for the same reason: they, Scripture and souls, are the primary fields of operation of the Holy Spirit. An interest in souls divorced from an interest in Scripture leaves us without a text that shapes these souls. In the same way, an interest in Scripture divorced from an interest in souls leaves us without any material for the text to work on.

By and large the Christian community accepts the position that the Bible is the authoritative text by which God reveals himself. I don't intend to argue that here; it has been well argued and thought-out by our theologians and Scripture scholars. My task is to bring into awareness and focus what is on the other side of the coin, that this Scripture text, in the course of revealing God, pulls us into the revelation and welcomes us as participants in it. What I want to call attention to is that the Bible, all of it, is *livable;* it is *the* text for living our lives. It reveals a God-created, God-ordered, God-blessed world in which we find ourselves at home and whole.

And I want to begin with the metaphor *Eat this book.* I want to recover the metaphor along with all its implications for the Christian community in which I live. I want to impress this command on the imagination of the Christian generation of which I am a part so that it takes an honored place in the company of great gospel commands that are clustered in the forefront of awareness among all who follow Jesus. Most of us carry around a handful of essential commands that keep us on track: "Love the Lord your God with all your heart. . . . Love your neighbor. . . . Honor your father and mother. . . . Repent and believe. . . . Remember the Sabbath. . . . Be not anxious. . . . Give thanks at all times. . . . Pray without ceasing. . . . Follow me. . . . Go and tell. . . . Take up your cross. . . ." Add this to your repertoire: Eat this book. Not merely Read your Bible but *Eat this book.*

*   *   *

Christians feed on Scripture. Holy Scripture nurtures the holy community as food nurtures the human body. Christians don't simply learn or study or use Scripture; we assimilate it, take it into our lives in such a way that it gets metabolized into acts of love, cups of cold water, missions into all the world, healing and evangelism and justice in Jesus' name, hands raised in adoration of the Father, feet washed in company with the Son.

The metaphorical imperative arrives among us backed by the authority of St. John the Theologian ("the Divine" in the King James Version).

I went to the angel and told him to give me the little scroll; and he said to me, "Take it, and eat; it will be bitter to your stomach, but sweet as honey in your mouth." And I took the little scroll from the hand of the angel and ate it; it was sweet as honey in my mouth, but when I had eaten it my stomach was made bitter. (Rev. 10:9-10)

Does that get our attention? St. John is a commanding figure. He was pastor of marginal, politically and economically powerless Christians in a society in which their commitment to following Christ branded them as criminals of the state. His task was to keep their identity focused and their lives Spirit-filled, their discipleship ardent, their hope fresh against formidable odds — the living, speaking, acting *Jesus* front and center in their lives. He didn't settle for mere survival, throwing them a plank to hang onto in the storm; he wanted them to *live*, really live — outlive everyone around them. This is what prophets and pastors and writers do, and it is never easy. No easier now than it was for John.

It was in the course of the apocalyptic extravaganza that John is so famous for — these wildly boisterous, rambunctious, and celebrative visions that came to him one Sunday morning as he was worshipping on the prison island of Patmos — just as he was approaching the midpoint in the sequence of vision-messages, that he saw a gigantic angel, one foot planted in the ocean and the other on the continent, with a book in his hand. From this comprehensive land-and-sea pulpit the angel was preaching from the book, a sermon explosive with thunder. This was a sermon no one would sleep through! John started to write down what he was hearing — he'd never heard a sermon like this one — but was then told not to. A voice told John to take the book from the huge angel, this God-Messenger preaching from his world-straddling pulpit. And so he did, he walked up to the angel and said, "Give me the book." The angel gave it to him, but then said, "Here it is; eat it. Eat this book. Don't just take notes on the sermon. Eat the book." And John did it. He put away his notebook and pencil. He picked up his knife and fork. He ate the book.

The imagery, as is all the imagery in St. John's Revelation, is complex, a fusion of images from Moses and the Prophets and Jesus. This vision of the preaching angel is full of reverberating resonances. But what appears most immediate and obvious is that the mighty angel is preaching from the Bible, the Holy Scriptures. The book that John ate was the Bible, or as much of the Bible as was written at that time. The word "book" (Greek *biblion,* which arrives in our language as "Bible") suggests that the message God gives to us has meaning, plot, and purpose. Writing a book involves ordering words in a purposeful way. These words make sense. We do not come to God by guesswork: God reveals himself. These scriptural words reveal the Word that created heaven and earth; they reveal the Word that became human flesh in Jesus for our salvation. God's word is written, handed down, and translated for us so that we can enter the plot. We hold these Bibles in our hands and read them so that we can listen and respond to these creating and saving words and get in, firsthand, on the creating and saving.

The act of eating the book means that reading is not a merely objective act, looking at the words and ascertaining their meaning. Eating the book is in contrast with how most of us are trained to read books — develop a cool objectivity that attempts to preserve scientific or theological truth by eliminating as far as possible any personal participation that might contaminate the meaning. But none of us starts out reading that way. I have a granddaughter right now who eats books. When I am reading a story to her brother, she picks another off of a stack and chews on it. She is trying to get the book inside her the quickest way she knows, not through her ears, but through her mouth. She doesn't make fine distinctions between ear and mouth — any opening will do to get it inside her. But soon she'll go to school and be taught that that's not the way to go about it. She'll be taught to get answers out of her book. She'll learn to read books in order to pass examinations, and having passed the exams, put the book on the shelf and buy another.

But the reading that John is experiencing is not of the kind that equips us to pass an examination. Eating a book takes it all in, assimilating it into the tissues of our lives. Readers become what they read. If Holy Scripture is to be something other than mere gossip about God, it must be internalized. Most of us have opinions about God that we are not hesitant to voice. But just because a conversation (or sermon or lecture) has the word "God" in it, does not qualify it as true. The angel does not instruct St. John to pass on information about God; he commands him to assimilate the word of God so that when he does speak, it will express itself artlessly in his syntax just as the food we eat, when we are healthy, is unconsciously assimilated into our nerves and muscles and put to work in speech and action.

Words — spoken and listened to, written and read — are intended to do something *in* us, give health and wholeness, vitality and holiness, wisdom and hope. Yes, *eat* this book.

St. John, as mentioned earlier, wasn't the first biblical prophet to eat a book as if it were a peanut butter sandwich. Six hundred years earlier Ezekiel had been given a book and commanded to eat it (Ezek. 2:8–3:3). Ezekiel's contemporary, Jeremiah, also ate God's revelation, his version of the Holy Bible (Jer. 15:16). Ezekiel and Jeremiah, like John, lived in a time in which there was widespread pressure to live by a very different text than the one revealed by God in these Holy Scriptures. The diet of Holy Scripture for all three of them issued in sentences of tensile strength, metaphors of blazing clarity, and a prophetic life of courageous suffering. If we are in danger (which we certainly are) of succumbing to the widespread setting-aside of the Holy Scriptures and the replacing of them with the text of our own experience — our needs and wants and feelings — for authoritative direction in our actual day-by-day living, these three rough-and-tumble prophets — John, Ezekiel, Jeremiah — responsible for the spiritual formation of God's people in the worst of times (Babylonian exile and Roman persecution) ought to be able to convince us of their gut-level necessity: Yes, eat this book.

The Christian community has expended an enormous amount of energy and intelligence and prayer in learning how to "eat this book" after the manner of John on Patmos, Jeremiah in Jerusalem, and Ezekiel in Babylon.[2] We don't have to know all of it to come to the Ta-

2. James Houston gives an account of this "energy and intelligence and prayer" in *The Act of Bible Reading*, ed. Elmer Dyck (Downers Grove, Ill.: InterVarsity, 1996), pp. 148-73.

ble, but it helps to know some of it, especially since so many of our contemporaries treat it as a mere aperitif. The strong angel's command is also an invitation. Come to the Table and eat this book, for every word in the book is intended to do something in us, give health and wholeness, vitality and holiness to our souls and body.

CHAPTER 3

Scripture As Text:
Learning What God Reveals

Our lives, that is, our experience — what we need and want and feel — are important in forming the Christ-life in us. Our lives are, after all, the stuff that is being formed. But they are not the text for directing the formation itself. Spirituality means, among other things, taking ourselves seriously. It means going against the cultural stream in which we are incessantly trivialized to the menial status of producers and performers, constantly depersonalized behind the labels of our degrees or our salaries. But there is far more to us than our usefulness and our reputation, where we've been and who we know; there is the unique, irreproducible, eternal, image-of-God *me*. A vigorous assertion of personal dignity is foundational to spirituality.

There is a sense in which we can never take ourselves too seriously. We are serious business indeed. We are "fearfully and wonderfully made" (Ps. 139:14 NRSV). But it is possible to conceive of ourselves too narrowly, for there is far more to us than our genes and hormones, our emotions and aspirations, our jobs and ideals. There is God. Most, if not all, of what and who we are has to do with God. If we try to understand and form ourselves by ourselves we leave out most of ourselves.

And so the Christian community has always insisted that Holy Scripture that reveals God's ways to us is necessary and basic to our formation as human beings. In our reading of this book we come to realize that what we need is not primarily informational, telling us things about God and ourselves, but formational, shaping us into our true being.

It is the very nature of language to form rather than inform. When language is personal, which it is at its best, it reveals; and revelation is always formative — we don't know more, we become more. Our best users of language, poets and lovers and children and saints, use words to *make* — make intimacies, make character, make beauty, make goodness, make truth.

The Revealing and Revealed God

We begin at the beginning. We call this book "revelation," God revealing himself and his ways to us, not so much telling us something, but *showing* himself. Books have authors. However we conceive the words to have gotten written on the pages of our Bibles, the Christian church has always held that God is somehow or other responsible for this book in a revelatory way, in contrast to a merely informational way. The authority of the Bible is immediately derived from the authorial presence of God. In other words, this is not an impersonal authority, an assemblage of facts or truths. This is not the bookish authority that we associate with legislation codified in a law library, or the factual authority of a textbook on mathematics. This is revelation, personally revealed — letting us in on something, telling us person to person what it means to live our lives as men and women created in the image of God.

The early Christian community was handed, ready-made, a Bible, what we now name the Old Testament, the Torah and Prophets and Writings that were normative for the Hebrew people. For the first generation or so those Hebrew scrolls were the Christian Bible. But then the writings of Paul and other leaders in the early Christian communities began to be circulated widely, and the stories of Jesus that provided content for the good news, the "gospel" that was being gladly and urgently preached and taught, were written down. These writings were recognized to be continuous with the Holy Scriptures that they were already honoring and believing, preaching from and teaching. It gradually became obvious to them that the two sets of writings were congruent with one another, that there was an "authorial" continuity between these Hebrew Scriptures that had been part of their tradition for so long and these new Gospels and letters that were emerging from the worshipping and witnessing Christians. The recognition took awhile; it didn't happen all at once. After all, it required a considerable readjustment of the imagination to put a slim book written by Mark in the same company as the massive five volumes of God's word attributed to Moses. It was a tall order to take Paul's letters written to upstart and untested groups of new Christian nobodies and place them on a par with the centuries-tested Psalms and magisterial Isaiah. Brilliantly written as Paul's letters were, that didn't seem likely to happen. But it did happen. The holy community ended up putting the two sets together, the two "testaments," making a single book out of them, our Holy Bible. In a hundred years or so, the early Christians had essentially the same Holy Bible that we have today.

Not everybody agreed on what was done: the vote was not unanimous. There were factions that wanted nothing to do with the old Hebrew scrolls. They argued that the God in evidence in those old books was not even remotely connected with the God revealed and preached by Jesus. And there were other factions (various groups of gnostics) who went to the other extreme — they wanted to include anything that looked good, that promised an "inside" message, from among the many spiritually uplifting texts being written. "Insider" and "uplift" spiritualities were as popular then as they are now. But bit by bit the Christian community sifted out the sensational and the silly and were bold to designate their consensus as God's word.

The Holy Trinity: Keeping It Personal

What is supremely significant for us right now in understanding how to read this text is what happened as they put these two sets of writings together. They started out with the Scriptures that were normative for God's people Israel. They soon acquired these new Gospels and letters written out of the newly formed Christian community. Now they had to account for the continuities they perceived in these very different sets of books.

In the course of their talking and writing the consensus that emerged was that embedded in all these differences and diversities there was a single voice and that this voice was personal, the voice of God revealing himself. They accounted for this personal, revealing quality by formulating what we now name the Trinity. Trinity is an imaginative construct for enabling us to keep the diversity of the revelation coherent and whole. This is not the place to engage in an extensive discussion of the Trinity; what I want to say in this context is that our ancestors came up with this concept, "trinity," in the process of reading these same Scriptures that we are reading, in order to maintain the sense of a single, personal voice, in the midst of all the voices.

By the fourth and fifth centuries the best minds of the church were concentrating on reading these Scriptures and understanding how God exercised his sovereignty personally and uniquely among us. Their formulation of the Holy Trinity is an incredible work of genius, large enough and detailed enough to both account for everything that God is and has done, is doing, and will do, and at the same time show that all of us, no matter who we are or what we do or where we are from, are included. They worked hard and long at this formulation, calling councils, writing books, arguing, preaching, lobbying, and, yes, fighting. It was important to get it right and they knew it. They knew it was not a job they could leave to scholarly theologians working in libraries — this was person-in-the-street stuff. It had to do with *living* right, not just thinking right, with keeping everything in these Bibles of ours personal and livable.

In essence, what they came up with was this: As we read these Scriptures, what we realize is that God has a stable and coherent identity: God is one. But God also reveals himself in various ways that at first don't always seem to fit together. There are three obvious ways in which we see God working and revealing himself: the Father (the entire world of creation is in the forefront here), the Son (here we're dealing with the mess of history invaded by Jesus Christ and his work of salvation), and the Spirit (the pulling of our lives into God's life is the experienced element in this). It is always the same God, but the "person" or the "face" or "voice" by which we receive the revelation varies.[1]

But here's the thing: every part of the revelation, every aspect, every form is *personal* — God is relational at the core — and so whatever is said, whatever is revealed, whatever is received is also personal and relational. There is nothing impersonal, nothing merely functional, everything from beginning to end and in between is personal. God is inherently and inclusively personal.

The corollary to that is that I, because I am a person, am personally involved in the revelation. Every word I hear, everything I see in my imagination as this story unfolds, involves me relationally, pulls me into participation, *matters* to my core identity, affects who I am and what I do.

What I want to emphasize is that Trinitarian thinking developed out of two or three hundred years of our mothers and fathers patiently, prayerfully, intelligently reading these two Testaments and gradually realizing that the differences weren't all that different. As they read and listened to these sentences of Isaiah and Paul, Moses and Mark, David and John, they realized that they were hearing the same voice, which they named the Word of God. And as they heard and listened to this voice, they also heard themselves *addressed* — addressed as persons who possessed dignity and purpose and freedom, persons capable of believing and loving and obeying.

The authorial character of the Holy Scriptures was established as personal in the persons of Father, Son, and Holy Spirit. Because it was personal it was also relational, which meant that all reading/listening of Holy Scripture required personal, relational, participatory reading/listening. This was accompanied by the realization that these Holy

---

1. Karl Barth prefers the term "mode of being or existence. . . . God is one in three modes of being, Father, Son, and Holy Spirit." See his *Church Dogmatics,* vol. 1: *The Doctrine of the Word of God* (Edinburgh: T. & T. Clark, 1936), part 1, p. 413.

Scriptures in which God was revealing everything of who God is, also included everything of who we are: there is comprehensiveness and personal participation on both sides, author and reader.

This may be the single most important thing to know as we come to read and study and believe these Holy Scriptures: this rich, alive, personally revealing God as experienced in Father, Son, and Holy Spirit, personally addressing us in whatever circumstances we find ourselves, at whatever age we are, in whatever state we are — me, you, us. Christian reading is participatory reading, receiving the words in such a way that they become interior to our lives, the rhythms and images becoming practices of prayer, acts of obedience, ways of love.

We must not, even for a moment, suppose that Trinity is something thought up by theologians to deal with advanced mysteries quite remote from the daily work of people like us who have babies and have to work for a living. No, it was the work of Christians like us (some of them maybe a little smarter than we are!) learning and teaching each other how to read their Bibles as fully and attentively and personally and responsively as they were able. They wanted to read in such a way that their lives became congruent with the text. Convinced that this text was the authority for living well both now and into eternity, they wanted to get it all and get it right.

Depersonalizing the Text

But not everyone reads the Bible this way or wants to read it this way. Many find it interesting for other reasons, are attracted to it for other uses. The Bible has acquired a lot of authority through the centuries, and it is thought to be useful or interesting or helpful in ways other than involving us in the revelation of God.

There have always been a considerable number of people, for instance, who are fascinated by the intellectual challenges posed by the Bible. If you have a curious mind and like to use it in demanding ways, you can hardly do better than become a scholar of Holy Scripture. Walk into any theological library and meander through the aisles of the carefully cataloged books that have been written on the Bible and the various books of the Bible and you are simply staggered. Pick a book off the shelf at random and you are almost certain to find yourself holding the evidence of a first-class mind who has been quarrying these sentences for truth and coming up with most impressive and interesting results. Language, history, culture, ideas, geography, poetry — you name it, the Bible has it. A person can spend a lifetime before this Bible — reading, studying, lecturing, and writing — and never exhaust it.

There are others who come to the Bible with a more practical bent: They want to live well and have their children and neighbors live well. They know that the Bible provides sound counsel and provides trustworthy directions for getting on in the world, which is popularly assumed to involve becoming healthy, wealthy, and wise. The Bible has a reputation for charting a sound course for both personal and social behavior, and these people want to benefit from it. People as a general rule are an intractable lot with a tendency to get into trouble. This Bible can keep us out of the ditch and on the straight and narrow.

And, of course, there are always a considerable number of people who read the Bible for what is often called inspiration. There are so many beautiful and comforting passages in the Bible. When we are lonely or in grief or wanting some words that get us out of the humdrum, what is there better than the Bible? The stirring Elijah stories, the grand rhythms of the Psalms, the artful thunder of Isaiah's preaching, the charming parables of Jesus, the charged energy of Paul's teaching. If you're after devotionally cozy Bible reading, you have to pick and choose a good bit — there are such huge chunks of it that either put you to sleep or keep you awake nights. But there are little crib sheets readily available at most Bible bookstores that tell you what parts of the Bible to read when you want to be comforted or consoled — or whatever your present disposition requires.

I don't want to be too hard on any one of these groups of Bible-readers, especially since I've spent considerable time in each group myself, but I do want to call attention to the conspicuous fact that in whatever group you find yourself, you will be *using* the Bible for *your* purposes, and those purposes will not necessarily require anything of you relationally. It is entirely possible to come to the Bible in total sincerity, responding to the intellectual challenge it gives, or for the moral guidance it offers, or for the spiritual uplift it provides, and not in any way have to deal with a personally revealing God who has personal designs on you.

Or to put it in the terms in which we started out: It is possible to read the Bible from a number of different angles and for various purposes without dealing with God as God has revealed himself, without setting ourselves under the authority of the Father, the Son, and the Holy Spirit who is alive and present in everything we are and do.

To put it bluntly, not everyone who gets interested in the Bible and even gets excited about the Bible wants to get involved with God.

But God is what the book is about. C. S. Lewis, in the last book he wrote, talked about two kinds of reading, the reading in which we use a book for our own purposes and the reading in which we receive the author's purposes. The first ensures only bad reading; the second opens the possibility to good reading:

> When we "receive" it we exert our senses and imagination and various other powers according to a pattern invented by the artist. When we "use" it we treat it as assistance for our own activities. . . . "Using" is inferior to "reception" because art, if used rather than received, merely facilitates, brightens, relieves or palliates our life, and does not add to it.[2]

That is why an awareness of what the church has formulated as the Holy Trinity is so important as we come to this book, the Bible. We read in order to get in on the revelation of God, who is so emphatically *personal;* we read the Bible the way it comes to us, not in the way we

2. C. S. Lewis, *An Experiment in Criticism* (Cambridge: University Press, 1961), p. 88. Lewis also provided this illustration: "The one [receiving] . . . is like being taken for a bicycle ride by a man who may know roads we have never yet explored. The other [using] is like adding one of those little motor attachments to our own bicycle and then going for one of our familiar rides."

come to it; we submit ourselves to the various and complementary operations of God the Father, God the Son, and God the Holy Spirit; we receive these words so that we can be formed now and for eternity to the glory of God.

The Replacement Trinity

A new twist on non-Trinitarian ways of reading the Bible has emerged in our times. It has reached the scale of an epidemic and requires special attention. It can be understood best, I think, as a replacement Trinity. Unlike the depersonalized readings of the text that we have just marked (intellectual, practical, inspirational), this way is very personal and also very Trinitarian, but also totally at odds with what is achieved while reading in submission to the authority of the Holy Trinity.

Trinitarian thinking/praying before Holy Scripture cultivates a stance and attitude that submits to being comprehensively formed by God in the way God comprehensively and personally reveals himself as Father, Son, and Holy Spirit in the Holy Scriptures. The alternative to that is taking charge of our own formation. The most popular way of conceiving this self these days is by understanding the self in a Trinitarian way. This way of self-understanding is not as an intellectual interested in ideas or as a moral being seeking a good life or as a soul looking for solitary solace, but as a divine self in charge of my self. And this divine self is understood as a Holy Trinity.

Here's how it works. It is important to observe that in the formulation of this new Trinity that defines the self as the sovereign text for living, the Bible is neither ignored nor banned; it holds, in fact, an honored place. But the three-personal Father, Son, and Holy Spirit is replaced by a very individualized personal Trinity of my Holy Wants, my Holy Needs, and my Holy Feelings.

We live in an age in which we have all been trained from the cradle to choose for ourselves what is best for us. We have a few years of apprenticeship at this before we are sent out on our own, but the training begins early. By the time we can hold a spoon we choose between half a dozen cereals for breakfast, ranging from Cheerios to Corn Flakes. Our tastes, inclinations, and appetites are consulted endlessly. We are soon deciding what clothes we will wear and in what style we will have our hair cut. The options proliferate: what TV channels we will view, what courses we will take in school, what college we will attend, what courses we will sign up for, what model and color of car we will buy, what church we will join. We learn early, with multiple confirmations as we grow older, that we have a say in the formation of our lives and, within certain bounds, the decisive say. If the culture does a thorough job on us — and it turns out to be mighty effective with most of us — we enter adulthood with the working assumption that whatever we need and want and feel forms the divine control center of our lives.

The new Holy Trinity. The sovereign self expresses itself in Holy Needs, Holy Wants, and Holy Feelings. The time and intelligence that our ancestors spent on understanding the sovereignty revealed in Father, Son, and Holy Spirit are directed by our contemporaries in affirming and validating the sovereignty of our needs, wants, and feelings.

My needs are non-negotiable. My so-called rights, defined individually, are fundamental to my identity. My need for fulfillment, for expression, for affirmation, for sexual satisfaction, for respect, my need to get my own way — all these provide a foundation to the centrality of *me* and fortify my self against diminution.

My wants are evidence of my expanding sense of kingdom. I train myself to think big because I am big, important, significant. I am larger than life and so require more and more goods and services, more things and more power. Consumption and acquisition are the new fruits of the spirit.

My feelings are the truth of who I am. Any thing or person who can provide me with ecstasy, with excitement, with joy, with stimulus, with spiritual connection validates my sovereignty. This, of course, involves employing quite a large cast of therapists, travel agents, gadgets and machines, recreations and entertainments to cast out the devils of boredom or loss or discontent — all the feelings that undermine or challenge my self-sovereignty.

In the last two hundred years a huge literature, both scholarly and popular, has developed around understanding this new Holy Trinity of Needs, Wants, and Feelings that make up the sovereign self. It amounts to an immense output of learning. Our new class of spiritual masters is composed of scientists and economists, physicians and psychologists, educators and politicians, writers and artists. They are every bit as intelligent and passionate as our earlier church theologians and every bit as religious and serious, for they know that what they come up with has enormous implications for everyday living. The studies they conduct and the instruction they provide in the service of the god that is us, the godhead composed by our Holy Needs, Holy Wants, and Holy Feelings, are confidently pursued and very convincing. It is very hard not to be convinced with all these experts giving their witness. Under their tutelage I become quite sure that I am the authoritative text for the living of my life.

We might suppose that the preaching of this new Trinitarian religion poses no great threat to people who are baptized in the threefold name of the Trinity, who regularly and prayerfully recite the Trinitarian Apostles' and Nicene creeds, who begin prayers with the invocation, "Our Father . . . ," who daily get out of bed to follow Jesus as Lord and Savior and frequently sing, "Come Holy Spirit, heavenly dove. . . ."

But this rival sovereignty is couched in such spiritual language, and we are so easily convinced of our own spiritual sovereignty, that it does catch our attention. The new spiritual masters assure us that all our spiritual needs are included in the new Trinity: our need for meaning and transcendence, our wanting a larger life, our feelings of spiritual significance — and, of course, there is plenty of space to make room for God, as much or as little as you like. The new Trinity doesn't get rid of God or the Bible, it merely puts them to the service of needs, wants, and feelings. Which is fine with us, for we've been trained all our lives to treat everyone and everything that way. It goes with the territory. It's the prerogative of sovereignty.

What has become devastatingly clear in our day is that the core reality of the Christian community, the sovereignty of God revealing himself in three persons, is contested and undermined by virtually everything we learn in our schooling, everything presented to us in the media, every social, workplace, and political expectation directed our way as the experts assure us of the sovereignty of self. These voices seem so perfectly tuned to us, so authoritatively expressed and custom-designed to show us how to live out our sovereign selves, that we are hardly aware that we have traded in our Holy Bibles for this new text, the Holy Self. And don't we still attend Bible studies and read our assigned verse or chapter each day? As we are relentlessly encouraged to consult our needs and dreams and preferences, we hardly notice the shift from what we have so long professed to believe.

The danger of installing the self as the authoritative text for living, at the same time that we are honoring the Holy Scriptures by giving them a prominent place on the shelf, is both enormous and insidious. None of us is immune to the danger.

That is why it is so urgent to revive the strong angel's command to St. John. If we want to keep our identity, if we want a text to live by that keeps us in the company of God's people, keeps us conversant with who he is and the way he works, we simply must eat this book.

*   *   *

The blunt reality is that for all our sophistication, learning, and self-study we don't know enough to run our lives. The sorry state of the lives of the many who have taken their own experience as the text for their lives is a damning refutation of the pretensions of the sovereignty of the self. We require a text that reveals what we cannot know by simply pooling the acquired knowledge of the ages. The book, the Bible, reveals the self-revealing God and along with that the way the world is, the way life is, the way we are. We need to know the lay of the land that we are living in. We need to know what is involved in this Country of the Trinity, the world of God's creation and salvation and blessing.

God and his ways are not what most of us think. Most of what we are told about God and his ways by our friends on the street, or read about him in the papers, or view on television, or think up on our own, is simply wrong. Maybe not dead wrong, but wrong enough to mess up the way we live. And this book is, precisely, revelation, a revealing of what we could never figure out on our own.

Without this text, firmly established at the authoritative center of our communal and personal lives, we will founder. We will sink into a swamp of well-meaning but ineffectual men and women who are mired unmercifully in our needs and wants and feelings.

Hoshia

A few years ago while in Israel, my wife and I were invited to an Orthodox Jewish synagogue for morning prayers. We were in the little Galilean village of Hoshia. It was seven-thirty in the morning. There were fourteen or fifteen boys and young men ranging in age from about twelve to seventeen, along with a scattering of older men. The boys were reading the Bible — it was a large scroll that two boys ceremoniously removed from its place ("the ark"), placed reverently on a reading desk, and unrolled to the place of the assigned reading for the morning. They handled it so reverently, so proudly. And then one of them read, but he only seemed to read for he had memorized it, the entire Torah, the first five books of the Bible. We later learned that all the boys had memorized it in its entirety — knew it by heart from beginning to end. And they were so unselfconscious about what they were doing, so boyish, so obviously comfortable and joyful in what they were doing.

When the service of prayers and readings was completed, a few of the boys stayed behind to talk to us. They were so proud of their synagogue and their scrolls, so pleased to be able to tell us what they were doing. They were the furthest things from reluctant schoolboys having to do their lessons, or pious schoolboys trying to impress God with their devotion. They were just boys, but boys who had discovered with delight how the Bible works in them, revealing a living God for their living, these Scriptures being digested within them as they came together every morning to eat the book.

We were moved by the joyful devotion of those boys to God's revelation to them in that scroll, by their not talking about but living the centrality and authority of these Holy Scriptures. And then even more deeply moved when we later talked over how many boys and girls and men and women in gatherings all over the world, hungry men and women, were doing the same thing, and how lucky we were to have had so many good meals with so many of them — hearty meals, soul-filling meals.

CHAPTER 4

Scripture As Form:
Following the Way of Jesus

The apocalyptic strong angel, taking the cosmos for his pulpit, one foot planted in the ocean and the other on land and holding the Bible in his hand, preached. He preached the word of God. The words written in the text were thunder in the ears of St. John.

John (you will recall) was impressed, grabbed his notebook and pencil, and started to write down what he had just heard. A voice from heaven told him not to write what he had heard, but to take the book and eat it. The words in the book had just been re-voiced, taken off the page and set in motion in the air where they could enter ears. When John started to take the message he had heard, the rolling thunder of those sentences reverberating through land and sea, and write it down, he was stopped short — why, that would be like taking the wind out of the words and flattening them soundless on paper. The preaching angel had just gotten them off the printed page, and now John was going to put them back again. No, says the heavenly voice — I want those words out there, creating sound waves, entering ears, entering lives. I want those words preached, sung, taught, prayed — *lived*.

The voice then tells John to take the book from the angel. He takes it and the angel tells him, "Eat this book": Get this book into your gut; get the words of this book moving through your bloodstream; chew on these words and swallow them so they can be turned into muscle and gristle and bone. And he did it; he ate the book.

*   *   *

I am using the metaphor "Eat this book" as a way of focusing on and clarifying what it means to have these Holy Scriptures and how the holy community has learned to eat them, receive them in a way that forms us into Christians, men and women created and saved and blessed by God the Father, God the Son, and God the Holy Spirit.

The previous chapter, "Scripture As Text: Learning What God Reveals," was an orientation in the personal, revelatory nature of Holy Scripture. All these words are person-to-person — the three-personed God addressing himself personally to us in our full capacity as persons-in-relationship. The Holy Trinity provided a way of understanding the irreducible personal and relational nature of this text, and affirmed that the only reading congruent with what is written is also personal and participatory.

In this chapter, "Scripture As Form: Following the Way of Jesus," I want to observe the way in which these personal words arrive in our lives and connect the Jesus way with the way in which we now live them. I want to attend to the way that the form of Scripture is also the form of our lives.

*   *   *

I begin with a poem by Wendell Berry, one of our century's wiser guides, in which he uses the small farm on which he lives and works as a metaphor for form as formative. For forty years, in a succession of novels and poems and essays, Berry has been re-ordering our Christian imaginations to cultivate totalities, to live life as a spiritually organic whole. In his poem "From the Crest" he works his metaphor in a way that invites reflection on the form of Holy Scripture as it gives form to the Christian life.

I am trying to teach my mind
to bear the long, slow growth
of the fields, and to sing
of its passing while it waits.

The farm must be made a form,
endlessly bringing together
heaven and earth, light
and rain building back again
the shapes and actions of the ground.[1]

What Berry sees in his farm as a form, I see in Scripture as a form. Think of the farm as an organic whole, but with boundaries so that you are aware and stay in touch with all the interrelations: the house and barn, the horses and the chickens, the weather of sun and rain, the food prepared in the house and the work done in the fields, the machinery and the tools, the seasons. There are steady, relaxed rhythms in place.

I did not grow up on a farm but did grow up in farming country and was often on farms and ranches. My father was a butcher and so we were often on the farms buying and slaughtering beef and pork and lamb. I'm sure there are exceptions to this, but as I have thought through my early memories of being on those farms, I can't remember a farmer who was ever in a hurry. Farmers characteristically work hard, but there is too much work to do to be in a hurry. On a farm everything is connected both in place and in time. Nothing is done that isn't connected to something else; if you get in a hurry, break the rhythms of the land and the seasons and the weather, things fall apart — you get in the way of something set in motion last week or month. A farm is not neat — there is too much going on that is out of your control. Farms help us learn patience and attentiveness: "I am trying to teach my mind / to bear the long, slow growth / of the fields, and to sing / of its passing while it waits."

1. Wendell Berry, *Collected Poems* (San Francisco: North Point, 1985), pp. 190-91.

If anything or anyone is treated out of context, that is, isolated as a thing in itself apart from season or weather or soil conditions or the condition of the machinery or persons, it is violated: "The farm must be made a form, / endlessly bringing together / heaven and earth, light / and rain building back again / the shapes and actions of the ground."

Holy Scripture is a form in just this way: a fenced-in acreage of words and sentences of many different sorts and kinds, but all of them integral to the work that is being done, working in long, steady rhythms in which we, the readers, participate but don't control. We meditatively enter this world of words and give obedient and glad assent. We submit our lives to this text that is "endlessly bringing together / heaven and earth. . . ."

The Story

The text for Christian living, and therefore for spiritual theology, set within the spacious contours of this Jesus-welcoming, Spirit-anchored, God-defined, and Trinity-framed context, is the Bible, our Holy Scriptures. This Bible turns out to be a large, comprehensive story, a *metastory*. The Christian life is conducted in story conditions. The Bible is basically and overall a narrative — an immense, sprawling, capacious narrative.

Story is the primary verbal means of bringing God's word to us. For that we can be most grateful, for story is our most accessible form of speech. Young and old love stories. Literate and illiterate alike tell and listen to stories. Neither stupidity nor sophistication puts us outside the magnetic field of story. The only serious rival to story in terms of accessibility and attraction is song, and there are plenty of those in the Bible too.

But there is another reason for the appropriateness of story as a major means of bringing us God's word. Story doesn't just tell us something and leave it there, it invites our participation. A good storyteller gathers us into the story. We feel the emotions, get caught up in the drama, identify with the characters, see into nooks and crannies of life that we had overlooked, realize that there is more to this business of being human than we had yet explored. If the storyteller is good, doors and windows open. Our biblical storytellers, both Hebrew and Greek, were good in both the moral and aesthetic sense of that word.

Honest stories respect our freedom; they don't manipulate us, don't force us, don't distract us from life. They bring us into the spacious world in which God creates and saves and blesses. First through our imaginations and then through faith — imagination and faith are close kin here — they offer us a place in the story, invite us into this large story that takes place under the broad skies of God's purposes, in contrast to the gossipy anecdotes that we cook up on a hot plate in the stuffy closet of the self.

Not all stories, of course, are honest. There are sentimentalizing stories that seduce us into escaping from life; there are propagandistic stories that attempt to enlist us in a cause or bully us into a stereotyped response; there are trivializing stories that represent life as merely cute or diverting.

The Christian life requires a form adequate to its content, a form that is at home in the Christian revelation and that respects each person's dignity and freedom with plenty of room for all our quirks and particularities. Story provides that form. The biblical story invites us in as participants in something larger than our sin-defined needs, into something truer than our culture-stunted ambitions. We enter these stories and recognize ourselves as participants, whether willing or unwilling, in the life of God.

Unfortunately, we live in an age in which story has been pushed from its biblical frontline prominence to a bench on the sidelines and then condescended to as "illustration" or "testimony" or "inspiration." Our contemporary unbiblical preference, both inside and outside the church, is for information over story. We typically gather impersonal (pretentiously called "scientific" or "theological") information, whether doctrinal or philosophical or historical, in order to take things into our own hands and take charge of how we will live our lives. And we commonly consult outside experts to interpret the information for us. But we don't live our lives by information; we live them in relationships in the context of a personal God who cannot be reduced to formula or definition, who has designs on us for justice and salvation. And we live them in an extensive community of men and women, each person an intricate bundle of experience and motive and desire. Picking a text for living that is characterized by information-gathering and consultation with experts leaves out nearly everything that is uniquely *us* — our personal histories and relationships, our sins and guilt, our moral character and believing obedience to God. Telling and listening to a story is the primary verbal way of accounting for life the way we live it in actual day-by-day reality. There are no (or few) abstractions in a story. A story is immediate, concrete, plotted, relational, personal. And so when we lose touch with our lives, with our *souls* — our moral, spiritual, embodied God-personal lives — story is the best verbal way of getting us back in touch again. And that is why God's word is given for the most part in the form of story, this vast, overarching, all-encompassing story, this meta-story.

*   *   *

One of the characteristic marks of the biblical storytellers is a certain reticence. There is an austere, spare quality to their stories. They don't tell us too much. They leave a lot of blanks in the narration, an implicit invitation to enter the story ourselves, just as we are, and discover for ourselves how we fit into it. "The Scripture stories do not, like Homer's, court our favor, they do not flatter us that they may please us and enchant us — they seek to subject us, and if we refuse to be subjected we are rebels."[2]

The form in which language comes to us is as important as its content. If we mistake its form, we will almost certainly respond wrongly to its content. If we mistake a recipe for vegetable stew for a set of clues for finding buried treasure, no matter how carefully we read it, we will end up as poor as ever and hungry besides. If we mis-

2. Erich Auerbach, *Mimesis* (Princeton, N.J.: Princeton University Press, 1953), p. 15.

read a highway road sign, "Speed Limit 60," as a randomly posted piece of information rather than as a stern imperative, "Don't drive over 60 miles per hour!" we will eventually find ourselves pulled over on the side of the road with a police officer giving us a brief but expensive course in hermeneutics. Ordinarily, we learn these discriminations early and well, and give form and content equal weight in determining meaning.

But when it comes to Scripture we don't do nearly as well. Maybe it is because Scripture comes to us so authoritatively — *God's word!* — that we think all we can do is submit and obey. Submission and obedience are a large part of it, but first we have to listen. And listening requires listening to the *way* it is said (form) as well as to *what* is said (content).

Stories suffer misinterpretation when we don't submit to them simply as stories. We are caught off-guard when divine revelation arrives in such ordinary garb and mistakenly think it's our job to dress it up in the latest Paris silk gown of theology, or to outfit it in a sturdy three-piece suit of ethics before we can deal with it. The simple, or not so simple, story is soon, like David under Saul's armor, so encumbered with moral admonitions, theological constructs, and scholarly debates that it can hardly move. There are, of course, always moral, theological, historical elements in these stories that need to be studied and ascertained, but never in spite of or in defiance of the story that is being told.

One of many welcome consequences in learning to "read" our lives in the lives of Abraham and Sarah, Moses and Miriam, Hannah and Samuel, Ruth and David, Isaiah and Esther, Mary and Martha, Peter and Paul is a sense of affirmation and freedom: we don't have to fit into prefabricated moral or mental or religious boxes before we are admitted into the company of God; we are taken seriously just as we are and given a place in his story, for it is, after all, *his* story; none of us is the leading character in the story of our life.

Spiritual theology, using Scripture as text, does not present us with a moral code and tell us "Live up to this"; nor does it set out a system of doctrine and say, "Think like this and you will live well." The biblical way is to tell a story and in the telling invite: "Live *into* this —

43

this is what it looks like to be human in this God-made and God-ruled world; this is what is involved in becoming and maturing as a human being." We do violence to the biblical revelation when we "use" it for what we can get out of it or what we think will provide color and spice to our otherwise bland lives. That always results in a kind of "decorator spirituality" — God as enhancement. Christians are not interested in that; we are after something far bigger. When we submit our lives to what we read in Scripture, we find that we are not being led to see God in our stories but our stories in God's. God is the larger context and plot in which our stories find themselves.

* * *

We require a form that is large enough and resilient enough so that our formation as human beings is not constricted, so that we are not forced into something that is not *us*. We don't want to be stunted in our formation as we grow up in Christ, and we don't want to be forced into something that violates our image-of-God uniqueness.

But by restricting ourselves to a single book, the Bible, don't we risk just such deformations? Isn't there danger that we will outgrow this book? Isn't there danger that this old, old book will impose a way of life on us that we will experience as alien and coercive? Shouldn't we cover our bases with supplementary texts? There are a number of people around who object to the Bible as the authoritative text for our lives on the grounds that it is narrow, constrictive, and imposes a paternalistic worldview on us that we have long outgrown.

We want a spirituality that is world-embracing, all-experience–encompassing. Our sense of life is huge — we are in touch with Asians and Africans and Slavs, with Native Americans and South Americans. We are finding out about the remarkable spiritualities in Australian bush aborigines and the people of the South African Kalahari. How can we be satisfied to be people of one book?

But maybe we are putting the question wrongly. Perhaps we need to ask how we go about entering into a large life: Do we travel the world and pick up artifacts and souvenirs, bring them home and assemble a museum or workshop in which we can be in visual and sensory touch with as much as possible? Or is there another way to go about it? Does largeness come by acquisition of a lot of stuff from here and there, or by deepening into what is at hand? Do we form a spirituality text on analogy with multinational companies who make their mark by means of buyouts and takeovers, taking control but ignoring local culture and family relationships in order to turn everything they touch into the ultimate depersonalized abstraction, money? Or do we take what is right before us in our own backyard and sink our lives into what is already given to us, enter into the intricacies, the endless organic relationships that make up this world and live in this world? Henry David Thoreau, one of our canonized American sages, wrote of having "traveled a good deal in Concord"[3] (the small New England village in which he spent his life). An item in the oral tradition that formed around Louis Agassiz, the celebrated Harvard biologist and professor, remembers that he returned to his classroom after the summer vacation and told his students that he had spent the summer traveling and had made it halfway across his backyard. I want to hold out for traveling widely in Holy Scripture. For Scripture is the revelation of a world that is vast, far larger than the sin-stunted, self-constricted world that we construct for ourselves out of a garage-sale assemblage of texts.

But this largeness, this spaciousness, comes not from piling up details from the bookish study of Scripture but from a realization of its form. Hans Urs von Balthasar, the twentieth century's premier theologian in Christian spirituality, insisted that in matters of spirituality it is form that is formational:

> The content [Gehalt] does not lie behind the form [Gestalt] but within it. Whoever is not capable of seeing and "reading" the form will, by the same token, fail to perceive the content. Whoever is not illumined by the form will see no light in the content either.[4]

3. Henry David Thoreau, *Walden* (New York: New American Library, 1960), p. 7.
4. Hans Urs von Balthasar, *The Glory of the Lord*, vol. 1: *Seeing the Form*, trans. Erasmo Leiva-Merikakis (San Francisco: Ignatius, 1983), p. 151.

*   *   *

The story that is Scripture, broadly conceived, is the story of following Jesus. The Christian community has always read this story as not just one story among others but as the meta-narrative that embraces, or can embrace, all stories. If we fail to recognize the capaciousness of this form, we will almost certainly end up treating our biblical text anecdotally as "inspiration" or argumentatively as polemic.

The vast and embracing world of revelation to which our spirituality text gives witness is a narrative form that is badly served when we either atomize or privatize it. We obscure the form when we *atomize* Scripture by dissecting it, analyzing it like a specimen in the laboratory. Every detail of Scripture is worth pursuing endlessly; no scholarly attention expended over this text is ever wasted. But when the impersonal objectivity of the laboratory technician replaces the adoring dalliance of a lover, we end up with file drawers full of information, organized for our convenience as occasions present themselves. It ceases to function as revelation for us. Far too many contemporary spiritualities, as befits our technological age, are obsessed with technique. If the Christian Scriptures are treated as just another tool for enlightenment or access to the knowledge that is power, sacrilege has been committed. We also obscure the form when we *privatize* Scripture, using it for what we are wont to call "inspiration." Our Holy Scriptures, of course, are pervasively personal. We are personally commanded and blessed, rebuked and comforted, warned and guided. But personal is not the same as private. Privacy is possessive and isolating. The private is what is withdrawn from the common good for individual control or use or enjoyment; it is stealing. When we privatize Scripture we embezzle the common currency of God's revelation. But Scripture is never that — the revelation draws us out of ourselves, out of our fiercely guarded individualities, into the world of responsibility and community and salvation — God's sovereignty. "Kingdom" is the primary biblical metaphor for it.

And so the church community continues to insist on attending to this narrative form that is so powerfully and enduringly formative. Sometimes we're told that the Bible is a library made up of many kinds of writing: poems and hymns, sermons and letters, visions and dreams, genealogical lists and historical chronicles, moral teaching and admonition and proverbs. And, of course, story. But that is not the way it is. It is *all* embedded in story. Von Balthasar puts it this way: "The older contemplators of Scripture possessed the art of seeing the total form within individual forms and of bringing it to light from within them. But this naturally presupposes an understanding of totality that is spiritual and not literary. . . ."[5]

Nothing comes to us apart from the form. The Bible, the entire Bible, is "relentlessly narratival."[6] And we cannot change or discard the form without changing and distorting the content. This biblical narrative gathers everything into it, providing a beginning and ending, plot and character development, conflict and resolution. For most of the Christian centuries, attentive readers of the Bible have understood that its many voices and points of view are all contained in the narrative form and are given coherence by it. Instead of attempting to iron out the wrinkles of inconsistency and disharmony, we have to listen for resonances, echoes, patterns — the swarming complexity of lived truth, not pinned-down and labeled facts.

We also find ourselves in the story. This meta-narrative gathers us into the narrative. Good storytellers, by enlisting our imaginations, tease us into participation in the story they tell. When the storytelling is good, we are pulled into a world that is both truer and larger than the one we ordinarily occupy; but it is not an alien world. (The exception is escapist entertainment that deliberately falsifies by depersonalizing and manipulating reality — horror stories, harlequin romances, pornography, propaganda.) Good storytelling involves us in what has been sitting right in front of us for years but we hadn't noticed or hadn't thought was important or hadn't thought had anything to do with us. And then we do notice — the story wakes us up to what is *there* and has always been there. Without leaving the world in which we daily work and sleep and

5. von Balthasar, *The Glory of the Lord*, p. 550.
6. Walter Brueggemann, *Theology of the Old Testament* (Minneapolis: Fortress, 1997), p. 206.

play, we find ourselves in a far larger world; we embrace connections and meanings and significance in our lives far beyond what our employers and teachers, our parents and children, our friends and neighbors have told us, to say nothing of what is conveyed by the experts and celebrities with whom we anxiously surround ourselves. The Scriptures, simply by virtue of their narrative *form*, draw us into a reality in which we find ourselves in touch with the very stuff of our humanity; what we sense in our bones *counts*. It is a story large with the sense of God, a world suffused with God, a world permeated with God's spoken and unspoken word, his unseen and perceived presence, in such a way that we know that it is the world we were made for, the world in which we most truly belong. It isn't long before we find ourselves imaginatively (imagination and faith are, again, close kin here) entering the story, taking our place in the plot, and following Jesus.

We live today in a world impoverished of story; so it is not surprising that many of us have picked up the bad habit of extracting "truths" from the stories we read: we summarize "principles" that we can use in a variety of settings at our discretion; we distill a "moral" that we use as a slogan on a poster or as a motto on our desk. We are taught to do this in our schools so that we can pass examinations on novels and plays. It is no wonder that we continue this abstracting, story-mutilating practice when we read our Bibles. "Story" is not serious; "story" is for children and campfires. So we continuously convert our stories into the "serious" speech of information and motivation. We hardly notice that we have lost the form, the form that is provided to shape our lives largely and coherently. Our spirituality-shaping text is reduced to disembodied fragments of "truth" and "insight," dismembered bones of information and motivation.

Again: the way the Bible is written is every bit as important as what is written in it: narrative — this huge, capacious story that pulls us into its plot and shows us our place in its development from beginning to ending.[7] It takes the whole Bible to read any part of the Bible.

7. There is a congruence between the three-personal, Holy Trinity originating presence, comprehensive and coherent (as noted in Chapter 3), and the narrative form

Every sentence is embedded in story and can no more be understood accurately or fully apart from the story than any one of our sentences spoken throughout the course of the day can be understood apart from our relationships and culture and the various ways in which we speak to our children and parents, our friends and enemies, our employers and employees — and our God. Northrop Frye, who has so well taught us to read the Bible largely, wrote that

> the immediate context of the sentence [any sentence in Scripture] is as likely to be three hundred pages off as to be the next or preceding sentence. Ideally, every sentence is the key to the whole Bible. This is not a factual statement about the Bible, but it helps to explain the practice of preachers who knew what they were doing, like some of those in seventeenth-century England. In the sermons of John Donne, for example, we can see how the text leads us, like a guide with a candle, into the vast labyrinth of Scripture, which to Donne was an infinitely bigger structure than the cathedral he was preaching in.[8]

The Sentence

The story that locates us in the large world of God and that enlists us in following Jesus is told sentence by sentence. Walking and following, for the most part, doesn't require deliberate thought; it employs conditioned reflexes, muscle and nerve coordination acquired in the first few years of life. We walk without having to think about putting one step before another. We read a story the same way, the sentences unfolding one after the other without us having to stop and ponder each period or verb tense.

---

that we observe in our Scriptures. Dorothy Sayers is lavish with insights on this in her *The Mind of the Maker* (San Francisco: Harper and Row, 1941).

8. Northrop Frye, *The Great Code* (New York: Harcourt Brace Jovanovich, 1982), pp. 208-9.

But just as in walking without thinking we sometimes take a wrong turn, have to retrace our steps and recalculate our directions, and just as when we walk without thinking someone sometimes steps in and alerts us to a multitude of important details — flowers, birds, faces — we had missed along the way, and stops us so that we look around, amazed at what we had missed, so also in the reading of our Holy Scriptures.

As we make our way through this story, finding our lives in this story, following Jesus, we find ourselves from time to time stopping, or being stopped, and paying attention to the details that make up the story. We attend to the language, to the sentences that bring words into relationship with one another and into relationship with us. Words are never mere words — they convey spirit, meaning, energy, and truth. Exegesis is the discipline of attending to the text and listening to it rightly and well.

Exegesis introduces another dimension into our relation to this text. The text as story carries us along, we are in on something larger than ourselves, we let the story take us where it will. But exegesis is focused attention, asking questions, sorting through possible meanings. Exegesis is rigorous, disciplined, intellectual work. It rarely feels "spiritual." Men and women who are, as we say, "into" spirituality, frequently give exegesis short shrift, preferring to rely on inspiration and intuition. But the long and broad consensus in the community of God's people has always insisted on a vigorous and meticulous exegesis: Give long and close and learned attention to this text! All our masters in spirituality were and are master exegetes. There's a lot going on here; we don't want to miss any of it; we don't want to sleepwalk through this text.

A sentence of words is a marvelous thing. Words reveal. We are presented with reality, with truth that makes our world larger, our relations richer. Words get us out of ourselves and into a responsive relation with a larger world of time and space, things and people.

But a sentence of words is also a most mysterious thing. Words conceal. Words can be used to falsify and mislead. All of our experience with language is "after Babel." Much of our experience with language is with its misuse. We cannot assume that any word that we assume we know is identical with that same word when it occurs in the text. And it is disconcerting to find that a word that is used one way on page 26 is used in quite a different way on page 72.

Not only that, but language is constantly changing, in constant flux. If a word was used one way last week, it cannot be depended upon to be used the same way next week. And we have two and three thousand years of "weeks" separating us from the biblical text. Dictionaries never quite catch up.

Because of all this, exegesis cannot be slighted. The scriptural text is complex and demanding. The primary witnesses to God's revelation are the Old and New Testaments: Torah and Prophets and Writings in the Old Testament, Gospels and Letters and Apocalypse in the New. And written in Hebrew and Aramaic and Greek, languages that have, as all languages do, their own peculiar way of inflecting nouns, conjugating verbs, inserting prepositions in odd places, and arranging words in a sentence. Written on parchment and papyri. Written with pen and ink. Written in Palestine and Egypt and Syria and Greece and Italy.

Not all of us have to know all of this in order to read Holy Scripture formationally. But we do need to learn to pay attention in and around us as we follow Jesus. Exegesis is not in the first place a specialist activity of scholars, although we very much need these scholars working on our behalf. We are not, after all, deciphering hieroglyphics, as some would have us think. Exegesis is simply noticing and responding adequately (which is not simple!) to the demand that words make on us, that *language* makes on us.

The Reformers insisted on what they called the "perspicuity" of Scripture, that the Bible is substantially intelligible to the common person and requires neither pope nor professor to interpret it. It is essentially open to our understanding without recourse to academic specialists or a privileged priesthood. As the *Westminster Confession* says, "those things which are necessary to be known, believed, and observed for salvation, are so clearly propounded and opened in some place of Scripture or other, that not only the learned, but the unlearned, in a due course of the ordinary means, may attain unto a sufficient under-standing of them."[9] Roman Catholic scholar Hans Urs von Balthasar joins the Reformers regarding the perspicuity of Scripture, adamant in his insistence that "God's word is simple and clear, and no-one should let himself be turned from a direct uninhibited contact with the word, or allow his contact with it to be dimmed and dulled, by problems and mental reservations aroused by the thought that scholars interpret a text quite differently and more accurately than he can."[10]

But that doesn't mean that much care is not required. Each book has its own way about it, and generally a careful reader begins to learn how to read a book by slowly and carefully poking around in it for a very long time until he finds his or her way. A careful reader (an exe-gete!) will proceed with caution, allowing the book itself to teach us how to read it. For it soon becomes obvious that our Holy Scriptures are not composed in a timeless, deathless prose, a hyper-spiritual angel language with all the quirks and idiosyncrasies of local history and peasant dialect expunged. There are verbs that must be accurately parsed, cities and valleys to be located on a map, and long-forgotten customs to be comprehended.

This is an enormous inconvenience, particularly to those of us who feel an inclination and aptitude toward the spiritual. It is almost impossible for those of us who have picked up the word "spiritual" from hanging around church parking lots or clicking on the Internet not to feel that our attraction to the spiritual confers a slight edge of privilege to us, exempting us from the bother of exegesis. We sense that we are insiders to the ways of God; we get intuitions that confirm our ideas and insights. After that happens a few times, we feel we've graduated from tedious recourse to lexicons and grammars. We are, after all, initiates to the text who cultivate the art of listening to God whisper between the lines. It isn't long, as newspaper columnist Ellen Goodman once put it, before we're using the Bible more as a Ror-

9. *The Westminster Confession* I.vii.

10. Hans Urs von Balthasar, *Prayer,* trans. A. V. Littledale (London: Geoffrey Chapman, 1963), p. 179.

schach test than as a religious text, reading more ink into the text than we read out of it.[11] It isn't long before we're using the word "spiritual" to refer primarily to ourselves and our ideas, and only incidentally and by the way to God.

But, inconvenient or not, we are stuck with the necessity of exegesis. We have a written word to read and attend to. It is God's word, or so we believe, and we had better get it right. Exegesis is the care we give to getting the words right. Exegesis is foundational to Christian spirituality. Foundations disappear from view as a building is constructed, but if the builders don't build a solid foundation, their building doesn't last long.

Because we speak our language so casually, it is easy to fall into the habit of treating it casually. But language is persistently difficult to understand. We spend our early lives learning the language, and just when we think we have it mastered our spouse says, "You don't understand a thing I'm saying, do you?" We teach our children to talk, and just about the time we think they might be getting it, they quit talking to us; and when we overhear them talking to their friends, we find we can't understand more than one out of every eight or nine words they say. A close relationship doesn't guarantee understanding. A long affection doesn't guarantee understanding. In fact, the closer we are to another and the more intimate our relations, the more care we must exercise to hear accurately, to understand thoroughly, to answer appropriately.

Which is to say, the more "spiritual" we become, the more care we must give to exegesis. The more mature we become in the Christian faith, the more exegetically rigorous we must become. This is not a task from which we graduate. These words given to us in our Scriptures are constantly getting overlaid with personal preferences, cultural assumptions, sin distortions, and ignorant guesses that pollute the text. The pollutants are always in the air, gathering dust on our Bibles, corroding our use of the language, especially the language of faith. Exegesis is a dust cloth, a scrub brush, or even a Q-tip for keeping the words clean.

11. Ellen Goodman, in *The Baltimore Sun*, June 15, 1979.

It is useful for readers of the Bible to keep company with some of our master exegetes; the easiest way to do it is to use their commentaries. Biblical commentaries are, for the most part, employed by pastors or teachers in the preparation of sermons or lectures. They are treated as "tools." But there are treasures in these books for the ordinary reader of the Bible. Among those of us who read — eat — this text not in preparation for an assignment, but simply for direction and nourishment in following Jesus, which means most of us, biblical commentaries have for too long been overlooked as common reading for common Christians.

I recommend reading commentaries in the same way we read novels, from beginning to end, skipping nothing. They are, admittedly, weak in plot and character development, but their devout attention to words and syntax is sufficient. Plot and character — the plot of salvation, the character of Messiah — are everywhere implicit in a commentary and persistently assert their presence even when unmentioned through scores, even hundreds, of pages. The power of these ancient nouns and verbs century after century to call forth intelligent discourse from learned men and women continues to be a staggering wonder.

Among those for whom Scripture is a passion, reading commentaries has always seemed to me analogous to the gathering of football fans in the local bar after the game, replaying in endless detail the game they have just watched, arguing (maybe even fighting) over observations and opinion, and lacing the discourse with gossip about the players. The level of knowledge evident in these boozy colloquies is impressive. These fans have watched the game for years; the players are household names to them; they know the fine print in the rulebook and pick up every nuance on the field. And they care immensely about what happens in the game. Their seemingly endless commentary is evidence of how much they care. Like them, I relish in a commentary not bare information but conversation with knowledgeable and experienced friends, probing, observing, questioning the biblical text. Absorbed by this plot that stretches grandly from Genesis to Revelation, captured by the messianic presence that in death and resurrection saves us one and all — there is so much to notice, so much to talk over.

Not all commentaries fill the bill — some of them are written by scholars who seem to have no interest either in God or the story, but there are enough that qualify to convince me that they provide welcome and indispensable companionship to all of us readers of the text who, as we follow Jesus, don't want to miss anything along the way.[12]

*   *   *

Too many Bible readers assume that exegesis is what you do after you have learned Greek and Hebrew. That's simply not true. Exegesis is nothing more than a careful and loving reading of the text in our mother tongue. Greek and Hebrew are well worth learning, but if you haven't had the privilege, settle for English. Once we learn to love this text and bring a disciplined intelligence to it, we won't be far behind the very best Greek and Hebrew scholars. Appreciate the learned Scripture scholars, but don't be intimidated by them.

Exegesis is the furthest thing from pedantry; exegesis is an act of love. It loves the one who speaks the words enough to want to get the words right. It respects the words enough to use every means we have to get the words right. Exegesis is loving God enough to stop and listen carefully to what he says. It follows that we bring the leisure and attentiveness of lovers to this text, cherishing every comma and semicolon, relishing the oddness of this preposition, delighting in the surprising placement of this noun. Lovers don't take a quick look, get a "message" or a "meaning," and then run off and talk endlessly with their friends about how they feel.

*   *   *

Not that there are not so-called exegetes who do just that: treat the Bible as if it were a warehouse of information, oblivious to the obvious — that it is given to us in the form of a story that is intended to shape

12. I have suggested several of the commentaries I value highly in chapter 15 of *Take and Read* (Grand Rapids: Eerdmans, 1996).

our entire lives into the story of following Jesus, a life lived to the glory of God.

A hundred and fifty years ago, when such arid and depersonalized — de-storied — knowledge was a pall on the spiritual life of England, George Eliot created the character of Casaubon (in her novel *Middlemarch*) to pillory this sacrilege of intellect. Casaubon was a scholarly priest in the Anglican Church obsessed with mastering religious knowledge and then writing what he mastered. Dorothea Brooke, a young woman bursting with idealism and vitality, married him intending to assist him in what she thought of as his noble pursuit. But there was no life in the books that Casaubon studied and wrote — they were dead words without connection with anything or anyone living, least of all his ardent, exuberant, life-affirming wife. It took only a few weeks for Dorothea to realize that she had married a cadaver.

George Eliot's contemporary, Robert Browning, trumped her novel with his poem "A Grammarian's Funeral," mocking the pretentious but lifeless old exegete who "decided not to Live but Know." He "settled *Hoti*'s business — let it be! — / Properly based *Oun* — / Gave us the doctrine of the enclitic *De* / Dead from the waist down."[13]

More recently, Marianne Moore used the metaphor of a steamroller (in her poem, "To a Steamroller") to expose this heavy-handed and spiritless violation of the text:

The illustration
is nothing to you without the application.
    You lack half wit. You crush all the particles down
      into close conformity, and then walk back and forth on them.

Sparkling chips of rock
are crushed down to the level of the parent block.
    Were not "impersonal judgment in aesthetic
      matters, a metaphysical impossibility," you

13. Robert Browning, *The Poems and Plays* (New York: Modern Library, 1934), p. 169.

might fairly achieve
  it. As for butterflies, I can hardly conceive
    of one's attending upon you, but to question
    the congruence of the complement is vain, if it exists.[14]

Marianne Moore's brother was a pastor in a Presbyterian church in Brooklyn, and she worshipped in his congregation every Sunday morning. She probably wasn't referring to him as the "steamroller" — all the indications are that she had a warm appreciation for his preaching and pastoral work — but through him she had access to the dominant mind-set among pastors and scholars at the time (the 1930s) who were contemptuous of all the lively detail and intricacy of the words and sentences in our Holy Scriptures, and instead forced them into the service of a doctrine or a cause: "You crush all the particles [read "words"] down / into close conformity, and then walk back and forth on them," steamrollering the text into a road that is all surface, usable, practical, doctrinal. And dead.

But exegesis does not mean mastering the text, it means submitting to it as it is given to us. Exegesis doesn't take charge of the text and impose superior knowledge on it; it enters the world of the text and lets the text "read" us. Exegesis is an act of sustained humility: There is so much about this text that I don't know, that I will never know. Christians keep returning to it, with all the help we can get from grammarians and archaeologists and historians and theologians, letting ourselves be formed by it.

Yes, humility. For the more we learn and the more knowledge we acquire — especially when it is biblical knowledge, God-knowledge — the more liable we are to the temptation of going off on our own with our wonderful knowledge and using what we know to run our lives and other people's lives the way we want. But this text was never intended to train us and equip us into competence, graduate us into an expertise that establishes us as a superior class of Christians, certified and sent off to do God's work for him among the biblically unwashed.

14. Marianne Moore, *The Complete Poems* (New York: Macmillan, 1967), p. 84.

If the knowledge we acquire through our reading and study of this text that involves us in following Jesus, diverts us from the very Jesus we started out following, we would have been better off never to have opened the book in the first place.

But without exegesis, spirituality gets sappy, soupy. Spirituality without exegesis becomes self-indulgent. Without disciplined exegesis spirituality develops into an idiolect in which I define all the key verbs and nouns out of my own experience. And prayer ends up limping along in sighs and stutters.

Century after century exegetical techniques in the Christian community have been honed and our methodologies improved. It is an immense irony that a generation that has access to the best in biblical exegesis is, even among the so-called "educated clergy," so largely indifferent to it.

*   *   *

The story gives form to the sentences; the sentences provide content to the story. Following Jesus requires that they hold together, thoroughly integrated. Without the story form, the sentences in the Bible, the Bible verses, function as an encyclopedia of information from which we select whatever we need at the moment. Without the precisely crafted sentences the story gets edited and revised by seductive suggestions from some and by bullying urgencies from others, none of whom seems to have much interest in following Jesus. But it was to make us followers of Jesus that this text was given to us in the first place, and if either the large story or the detailed sentences are ever used for anything else, however admirable or enticing, why bother?

CHAPTER 5

Scripture As Script:
Playing Our Part in the Spirit

"Eat this book" is my metaphor of choice for focusing attention on what is involved in reading our Holy Scriptures formatively, that is, in such a way that the Holy Spirit uses them to form Christ in us. We are not interested in knowing more but in becoming more.

The task is urgent. It is clear that we live in an age in which the authority of Scripture in our lives has been replaced by the authority of the self: we are encouraged on all sides to take charge of our lives and use our own experience as the authoritative text by which to live.

The alarming thing is how extensively this spirit has invaded the church. I more or less expect the unbaptized world to attempt to live autonomously. But not those of us who confess Jesus as Lord and Savior. I am not the only one to notice that we are in the odd and embarrassing position of being a church in which many among us believe ardently in the authority of the Bible but, instead of submitting to it, use it, apply it, take charge of it endlessly, using our own experience as the authority for how and where and when we will use it.

One of the most urgent tasks facing the Christian community today is to counter this self-sovereignty by reasserting what it means to live these Holy Scriptures from the inside out, instead of using them for our sincere and devout but still self-sovereign purposes.

*   *   *

God speaks. When God speaks things happen. Holy Scripture opens with the words, "God said . . ." ringing out eight times, and after each sounding we see, piece by piece, one after another, elements of heaven and earth coming into being before our eyes and then climaxing in man and woman formed in the image of God. Psalm 33 compresses Genesis 1 into a sentence: "For he spoke, and it came to be . . ." (Ps. 33:9). That sets the stage for everything that follows in our Bibles, this profuse outpouring of commands and promises, blessings and invitations, rebukes and judgments, directing and comforting that makes up our Holy Scriptures.

My metaphor of choice, Eat this book, is from St. John. We have three sorts of John books in our New Testaments that take particular delight in presenting Jesus as the one who reveals the God-speaking, word-of-God core and origin of everything that is: the Gospel of John, the letters of John, and the Apocalypse of John. It is by no means certain (although early tradition held it so) that the apostle John authored all these books; what is plain enough, though, is that all of them work out of a common center and emphasis — they are all *Johannine*. Jesus, the Word made flesh, speaks sentences that transform chaos into cosmos (the Gospel), sin into salvation (the letters), and brokenness into holiness (the Apocalypse).

St. John's Gospel opens with this emphatically verbal beginning, repeating "word" three times: "In the beginning was the Word, and the Word was with God, and the Word was God . . ." (John 1:1). This Word, we soon find out, is Jesus: "And the Word became flesh and dwelt among us, full of grace and truth; we have beheld his glory" (John 1:14). The Gospel story proceeds to present Jesus speaking reality into existence.

The letters of St. John likewise go back to the beginning and give witness to the apostolic experience of being convinced that that "word of life" was Jesus, verified by what they heard, what they saw, and what they touched. Three of our five senses (seeing, hearing, touching) are employed in the verification (1 John 1:1). This Jesus spoke the commands that resulted in a life of salvation from sin expressed in a community of love.

And, finally, the Apocalypse of St. John presents the risen and present Jesus, under the aspect of words, of speech: John gives "witness to the word of God and to the testimony of Jesus Christ" (Rev. 1:2). This risen Jesus Christ then identifies himself to John alphabetically, "I am Alpha and Omega" — he is the alphabet, all the letters from A to Z, that is, the stuff, the vowels and consonants out of which all words are made. Jesus speaks in such ways that the brokenness of the world and our experience develop into a dazzling holiness that evokes worship on a grand scale, involving everything and everyone in heaven and on earth.

Language is the primary way in which God works. In the Scriptures that give witness to these words this language is referred to in very physical ways. We hear the words, of course. But we also see the words ("I turned to see the voice," Rev. 1:12), chew them (Ps. 1:2), taste them (Ps. 19:10), walk and run in them (Ps. 119:32), and, in this final image, we eat them: Eat this book. This word of God that forms us in Christ is very physical.

We are part of a holy community that for three thousand years and more has been formed inside and out by these words of God, words that have been heard, tasted, chewed, seen, walked. Reading Holy Scripture is totally physical. Our bodies are the means of providing our souls access to God in his revelation: eat this book. A friend reports to me that one of the early rabbis selected a different part of our bodies to make the same point; he insisted that the primary body part for taking in the word of God is not the ears but the feet. You learn God, he said, not through your ears but through your feet: follow the Rabbi.

And so it is the practice of the Christian community to cultivate habits of reading that sharpen our perceptions and involve us in getting this word of God formatively within us — wanting to do it as well as the best of our ancestors, determined not to leave any of these words in a book on a shelf, like a can of baked beans stored in a cupboard. We want to work up a good appetite, join St. John and eat this book.

Following the introductory matter of Chapters 1 and 2, in Chapter 3, "Scripture As Text: Learning What God Reveals," the emphasis was on the Holy Trinity, that God reveals himself personally and relationally. Language is not primarily informational but revelatory. The Holy Scriptures give witness to a living voice sounding variously as Father, Son, and Spirit, addressing us personally and involving us personally as participants. This text is not words to be studied in the quiet preserves of a library, but a voice to be believed and loved and adored in workplace and playground, on the streets and in the kitchen. Receptivity is required.

In Chapter 4, "Scripture As Form: Following the Way of Jesus," the emphasis was on following Jesus into this wide-ranging but intricately coherent world that we become aware of by means of story. The Holy Scriptures are story-shaped. Reality is story-shaped. The world is story-shaped. Our lives are story-shaped. "I had always," wrote G. K. Chesterton in accounting for his Christian belief, "felt life first as a story: and if there is a story, there is a story-teller."[1] We enter this story, following the story-making, storytelling Jesus, and spend the rest of our lives exploring the amazing and exquisite details, the words and sentences that go into the making of the story of our creation, salvation, and life of blessing. It is a story chock full of invisibles and intricate with connections. Imagination is required.

And now in this chapter, "Scripture As Script: Playing Our Part in the Spirit," my emphasis is on the cultivation of understandings and practices that make us receptive listeners to the living Trinitarian voice that brought these words onto the pages of our text in the first place, but also brings them off the pages into our lives. The emphasis is on the cultivation of understandings and practices that make us better *followers* of Jesus into the story he speaks into being so that we find ourselves at home in it, both now and in eternity. Participation is required.

---

1. G. K. Chesterton, *Orthodoxy* (New York: Image, 1959), p. 61.

The Uncongenial Bible

We are delighted to find ourselves in this world of the biblical text. There is so much to explore, so much to learn — and to think that we have a place in this! It is not just about Ishmael and Isaac, Jacob and Esau, Zipporah and Asenath, David and Jonathan, Jeremiah and Ezekiel, Priscilla and Aquila, Rhoda and Phoebe, Barnabas and Mark — it is about me, and about you. Our parents and our children, our friends and enemies, our neighborhoods and our governments are all included.

A number of years ago I was in a bookstore. As I was paying for my purchase, I saw a stack of books on the counter. The book had been written by a good friend of mine. His name was prominent on the cover: Alvin ben-Moring. The book was about one of the wise men present at Jesus' birth. *Balthasar: The Black and Shining Prince* was the title. It was a popular Christmas book in the sixties. I hadn't seen Ben for several years, but I knew about this book. We had talked about this book, discussed plot and characters during the years we were together in college and seminary. And now here it was, published! I said to the clerk, "This book was written by a good friend of mine; I didn't know it had been published." She said, "Well, you'd better buy it; you might find yourself in it."

I did buy it, and I did find myself in it. But not in the way I expected. We had been close friends; he had given every indication of liking, even admiring, me. But in the book I was not at all likable, and certainly not admirable. There was no escaping the fact that it was me — unfortunately, though, not the me of my fantasies.

*   *   *

There is a detail in this story of John eating the book that I have ignored until now, but I can't avoid it any longer. This is the detail: eating the Bible gave John a stomachache.

It tasted good when he put it in his mouth, but when it got to his stomach he got sick on it: "I took the little scroll from the hand of the angel and ate it; it was sweet as honey in my mouth, but when I had eaten it my stomach was made bitter" (Rev. 10:10).

For most of us, our first experience with the Bible is sweet; we find ourselves in this book, and that is so wonderful. We acquire a taste for the promises and blessings of God, we learn to appreciate the sound counsel and direction for our lives, we memorize a few psalms that we can recite in dark and lonely times and find comfort. There is so much here to delight us. Psalm 119 uses an elaborate and exhaustive scheme, twenty-two stanzas that go through the twenty-two letters of the Hebrew alphabet, to celebrate the unending delight of God's word, coming to us in so many ways and forms. Each of the twenty-two eight-line stanzas contains eight synonyms for "word" or "God's word," reworking and reconfiguring them to give a sense of the complexity and diversity that radiate from God's speech. (A few variations in the eight synonyms show a certain freedom in composing the lines.) This amazing psalm convincingly conveys the pleasures the Holy Scriptures give us as the truths and promises and blessings sink into our lives word by word in meditation and prayer: "How sweet are thy words to my taste, sweeter than honey to my mouth" (Ps. 119:103). Dietrich Bonhoeffer wrote that in seminary he had been told that this was the most boring of the psalms;[2] but during his imprisonment by the Nazis he found that this was the richest psalm of all, and relished long meditations on it.[3]

But sooner or later we find that not everything is to our liking in this book. It starts out sweet to our taste; and then we find that it doesn't sit well with us at all; it becomes bitter in our stomachs. Finding ourselves in this book is most pleasant, flattering even; and then we find that the book is not written to flatter us, but to involve us in a reality, God's reality, that doesn't cater to our fantasies of ourselves.

There are hard things in this book, hard things to hear, hard things to obey. There are words in this book that are difficult to digest. John got a severe case of indigestion.

2. Artur Weiser's comment is typical: "a many-coloured mosaic of thoughts which are often repeated in a wearisome fashion." *The Psalms* (Philadelphia: Westminster, 1962), p. 739.

3. *Dietrich Bonhoeffer: Meditating on the Word*, ed. David McI. Grace (Cambridge, Mass.: Cowley, 1986), pp. 13-14.

But it is not just the hard sayings, it is the *way* the Bible comes to us. There are moments when it strikes us as totally strange, impossible to fit into our scheme of thinking and living. We try our best to domesticate this revelation, to fit it into our version of the way we would like things to be. Far too much of our so-called study of the Bible is an attempt to come up with explanations or programs that fit the Holy Trinity into our Holy Needs, Holy Wants, and Holy Feelings.

Every careful reader of the Bible is struck by how "recurringly odd and unaccommodating"[4] it is to what we are used to and expect. The Bible is "no easy read."[5]

It is far too common among us to develop a problem-solving habit of approach to the Bible, figuring out what doesn't seem to fit and then sanding off the rough edges, so that it slips into our ways of thinking more easily. We want to use it for comfort, and if it doesn't work comfortably we reconfigure it so that it will. One good friend warns his students against becoming expert text-nicians. Text-nicians learn this text, master it inside and out, so that they can repair it when we sense it's a little "off," so that it will run smoothly and get us where we want to go with our needs and wants and feelings.

But nothing in our Bibles is one-dimensional, systematized, or theologized. Everything in the text is intimately and organically linked to lived reality. We can no more diagram and chart the Bible into neatly labeled subjects or developments than we can our gardens. A garden is constantly changing with growth of both flowers and weeds. Or, to take a more complex comparison, think of a county fair crowded with carnival rides and sideshows, children clutching allowance money, farm animals on exhibit and horse races, men and women from every station of life. The place is charged with life, human and animal, good and bad, greedy and generous, indolent and determined. Such things, whether garden or county fair, can only be *entered*.

4. Walter Brueggemann, *Theology of the Old Testament* (Minneapolis: Fortress, 1997), p. 3.

5. Mark Coleridge, "Life in the Crypt or Why Bother with Biblical Studies," *Biblical Interpretation* 2 (July 1994): 148.

The Bible is a revelation of such lived reality, with God as the dominant form of life. Truths cannot be extracted from it — every detail must be taken as it comes to us in the text where it is found. "Every *what* is linked to a *how*," writes Walter Brueggemann; "we cannot generalize or summarize, but must pay attention to the detail"[6]

The most frequent way we have of getting rid of the puzzling or unpleasant difficulties in the Bible is to systematize it, organizing it according to some scheme or other that summarizes "what the Bible teaches." If we know what the Bible teaches, we don't have to read it anymore, don't have to enter the story and immerse ourselves in the odd and unflattering and uncongenial way in which this story develops, including so many people and circumstances that have nothing to do, we think, with us.

We are fond of saying that the Bible has all the answers. And that is certainly correct. The text of the Bible sets us in a reality that is congruent with who we are as created beings in God's image and what we are destined for in the purposes of Christ. But the Bible also has all the questions, many of them that we would just as soon were never asked of us, and some of which we will spend the rest of our lives doing our best to dodge. The Bible is a most comforting book; it is also a most discomfiting book. Eat this book; it will be sweet as honey in your mouth; but it will also be bitter to your stomach. You can't reduce this book to what you can handle; you can't domesticate this book to what you are comfortable with. You can't make it your toy poodle, trained to respond to your commands.

This book makes us participants in the world of God's being and action; but we don't participate on our own terms. We don't get to make up the plot or decide what character we will be. This book has generative power; things happen to us as we let the text call forth, stimulate, rebuke, prune us. We don't end up the same.

Eat this book, but also have a well-stocked cupboard of Alka-Seltzer and Pepto-Bismol at hand.

---

6. Brueggemann, *Theology of the Old Testament*, p. 55.

The Immense World of the Bible

Earlier (in Chapter 1) I referred to Karl Barth's reference to the "strange new world within the Bible." He passionately, relentlessly insisted that this is a book like no other book. Every expectation that we bring to this book is inadequate or mistaken. This is a text that reveals the sovereign God in being and action. It does not flatter us, it does not seek to please us. We enter this text to meet God as he reveals himself, not to look for truth or history or morals that we can use for ourselves. What he insisted upon supremely was that we do not read the Bible in order to find out how to get God into our lives, get him to participate in our lives. That's getting it backward.

As we cultivate a participatory mind-set in relation to our Bibles, we need a complete renovation of our imaginations. We are accustomed to thinking of the biblical world as smaller than the secular world. Tell-tale phrases give us away. We talk of "making the Bible relevant to the world," as if the world is the fundamental reality and the Bible something that is going to help it or fix it. We talk of "fitting the Bible into our lives" or "making room in our day for the Bible," as if the Bible is something that we can add on to or squeeze into our already full lives.

As we personally participate in the Scripture-revealed world of the emphatically personal God, we not only have to be willing to accept the strangeness of this world — that it doesn't fit our preconceptions or tastes — but also the staggering largeness of it. We find ourselves in a truly expanding universe that exceeds anything we learned in our geography or astronomy books.

Our imaginations have to be revamped to take in this large, immense world of God's revelation in contrast to the small, cramped world of human "figuring out." We learn to live, imagine, believe, love, converse in this immense and richly organic and detailed world to which we are given access by our Old and New Testaments. "Biblical" does not mean cobbling texts together to prove or substantiate some dogma or practice that we have landed on. Rather, it signals an opening up into what "no eye has seen, nor ear heard, nor the heart of man conceived, [but] what God . . . has revealed to us through the spirit" (1 Cor. 2:9-10).

What we must never be encouraged to do, although all of us are guilty of it over and over, is to force Scripture to fit our experience. Our experience is too small; it's like trying to put the ocean into a thimble. What we want is to fit into the world revealed by Scripture, to swim in this vast ocean.

What we are after is first noticing and then participating in the way the large world of the Bible absorbs the much smaller world of our science and economics and politics that provides the so-called world-view in which we are used to working out our daily concerns.

This means we have to abandon all condescending approaches to the Bible. Most of us have been trained in what is sometimes termed a "hermeneutics of suspicion." People lie a lot. And people who write lie more than most. We are taught to bring a healthy suspicion to every-thing we read, especially when it claims authority over us. And rightly so. We examine and cross-examine the text. What's going on here? What's the hidden agenda? What's behind all of this? The three mod-ern masters of the hermeneutic of suspicion are Nietzsche, Marx, and Freud. They taught us well to take nothing at face value.

Much of this is useful. We don't want to be taken in, manipulated by clever wordsmiths or enticed by skilled publicists and advertisers to buy things we don't want and will never use, involved in some soul-destroying program by a smooth-talking propagandist. In matters that have to do with God, we are doubly on our guard, suspicious of every-thing and everyone, including the Bible. We've learned to our sorrow that religious people lie more than most others — and lies in the name of God are the worst lies of all.

But as we narrow our eyes in suspicion, the world is correspond-ingly narrowed down. And when we take these reading habits to our reading of Holy Scripture, we end up with a small sawdust heap of facts.

Paul Ricoeur has wonderful counsel for people like us. Go ahead, he says, maintain and practice your hermeneutics of suspicion. It is im-portant to do this. Not only important, it is necessary. There are a lot of lies out there; learn to discern the truth and throw out the junk. But then reenter the book, the world, with what he calls "a second naiveté."[7] Look at the world with childlike wonder, ready to be startled into surprised delight by the profuse abundance of truth and beauty and goodness that is spilling out of the skies at every moment. Cultivate a hermeneutics of adoration — see how large, how splendid, how magnificent life is.

And then practice this hermeneutic of adoration in the reading of Holy Scripture. Plan on spending the rest of your lives exploring and enjoying the world both vast and intricate that is revealed by this text.

Obedience

We enter the world of the text, the world in which God is subject, in order to become participants in the text. We have our part to play in this text, a part that is given to us by the Holy Spirit. As we play our part we become *part*-icipants.

We are given this book so that we can imaginatively and believingly enter the world of the text and follow Jesus. John Calvin in his treatment of Holy Scripture is commonly cited in this regard: "all right knowledge of God is born of obedience."[8] There is hardly a Scripture exegete or translator of any standing in the Christian community who hasn't said the same thing.

If we have not entered this text as participants we aren't going to understand what is going on. This text cannot be understood by watching from the bleachers — or even from expensive box seats. We are in on it.

*   *   *

7. Paul Ricoeur, *The Symbolism of Evil* (Boston: Beacon, 1967), p. 351.

8. John Calvin, *Institutes of the Christian Religion*, ed. John T. McNeill, trans. Ford Lewis Battles (Philadelphia: Westminster, 1960), vol. 1, chap. 6, section 2.

The participatory quality of spiritual reading struck me forcibly when I was thirty-five years old. I had taken up running again. I had run in college and seminary and enjoyed it immensely, but when I left school, I left running. It never occurred to me that running was something an adult might do just for the fun of it. Besides, I was a pastor now and I wasn't sure how my parishioners would take to seeing their pastor running thinly clad along the back roads of our community. But I was noticing other people, doctors and lawyers and executives whom I knew, running in unexpected places without apparent loss of dignity, men and women my age and older, and realized that I could probably get by with it too. I went out and bought running shoes — Adidas, they were — and discovered the revolution in footwear that had taken place since my student days. I began having fun, enjoying again the smooth rhythms of long-distance running, the quietness, the solitude, the heightened senses, the muscular freedom, the texture of the ground under my feet, the robust embracing immediacy of the weather — wind, sun, rain, snow . . . whatever. Soon I was competing in 10K races every month or so, and then a marathon once a year. Running developed from a physical act to a ritual that gathered meditation, reflection, and prayer into the running. By this time I was subscribing to three running magazines and regularly getting books from the library on runners and running. I never tired of reading about running — diet, stretching, training methods, care of injuries, resting heart rate, endorphins, carbohydrate loading, electrolyte replacements — if it was about running I read it. How much is there to write about running? There aren't an infinite number of ways you can go about it — mostly it is just putting one foot before the other. None of the writing, with few exceptions, was written very well. But it didn't matter that I had read nearly the same thing twenty times before; it didn't matter if the prose was patched together with clichés; I was a runner and I read it all.

And then I pulled a muscle and couldn't run for a couple of months as I waited for my thigh to heal. It took me about two weeks to notice that since my injury I hadn't picked up a running book or opened a running magazine. I didn't *decide* not to read them; they were still all over the house, but I wasn't reading them. I wasn't reading because I wasn't running. The moment I began running again I started reading again.

That is when I caught the significance of the modifier "spiritual" in "spiritual reading." It meant participatory reading. It meant that I read every word on the page as an extension or deepening or correction or affirmation of something that I was a part of. I was reading about running not primarily to find out something, not to learn something, but for companionship and validation and confirmation of the experience of running. Yes, I did learn a few things along the way, but mostly it was to extend and deepen and populate the world of running that I loved so much. But if I wasn't running, there was nothing to deepen.

The parallel with reading Scripture seems to me almost exact: if I am not participating in the reality — the God reality, the creation/salvation/holiness reality — revealed in the Bible, not involved in the obedience Calvin wrote of, I am probably not going to be much interested in reading about it — at least not for long.

Obedience is the thing, living in active response to the living God. The most important question we ask of this text is not, "What does this mean?" but "What can I obey?" A simple act of obedience will open up our lives to this text far more quickly than any number of Bible studies and dictionaries and concordances.

Not that the study is not important. A Jewish rabbi I once studied with would often say, "For us Jews studying the Bible is more important than obeying it, because if you don't understand it rightly you will obey it wrongly and your obedience will be disobedience."

This also is true.

*   *   *

Anthony Plakados was a thirty-five-year-old truck driver in my congregation. Anthony grew up in a Greek home, conventionally Catholic, but none of it rubbed off. He left school after the eighth grade. He told me that he had never read a book. And then he became a Christian, got himself an old King James Bible with small print, and read it three times in that first year of his conversion. Anthony was off and running. Mary, his wife, was interested but also a bit bewildered by all this and asked a lot of questions. Mary had grown up a proper Presbyterian, gone to Sunday School all her growing up years, and was used to a religion of definitions and explanations. When Mary's questions got too difficult for Anthony, he would invite me to their trailer-house home, papered with Elvis Presley posters, to help him out. One evening the subject was the parables — Mary wasn't getting it. I was trying to tell her how to read them, how to make sense out of them. I wasn't getting on very well, and Anthony interrupted, "Mary, you got to live 'em, then you'll understand 'em; you can't figger 'em out from the outside, you got to git inside 'em — or let them git inside you."

And Anthony hadn't read so much as a word of John Calvin.

Reading Scripture Liturgically

I want to introduce a term now that may take some getting used to in this context: liturgy. As we eat this book, reading and responding and following, obeying and praying, as we take this all in and become participants in the text, we need help. We need the help of everyone and everything around us, for this is no private performance that we are engaged in, and we certainly are not the star of the show. "Liturgical" is the term I want to use to name the help we require. The Bible must be read liturgically.

To ward off confusion let me first say what I don't mean: by liturgy I don't mean what goes on in the chancel of a high Anglican church; I don't mean an order of worship; I don't mean robes and candles and incense and genuflections before the altar. Liturgy is properly used in all those settings, but I am after something else, I am after something deeper and higher and wider.

What I want to do is recontextualize our reading of Scripture, our eating of this book, into a huge holy community of others who are also reading it. There is a millennia-deep and globe-encircling community of others who are also at the table eating this book. Each time this book is assimilated formationally, the entire community — it is no exaggeration to say, the entire world — is involved and affected. The biblical story pulls the holy community — not just you, not just me — into the story in a participating way.

Liturgy is the means that the church uses to keep baptized Christians in living touch with the entire living holy community as it participates formationally in Holy Scripture. I want to use the word "liturgy" to refer to this intent and practice of the church insofar as it pulls everything in and out of the sanctuary into a life of worship, situates everything past and present coherently as participation in the revelation written for us in Scripture. Instead of limiting liturgy to the ordering of the community in discrete acts of worship, I want to use it in this large and comprehensive way, the centuries-deep and continents-wide community, spread out in space and time, as Christians participate in actions initiated and formed by the words in this book — our entire existence understood liturgically, that is, connectedly, in the context of the three-personal Father, Son, and Holy Spirit and furnished with the text of Holy Scripture.

The task of liturgy is to order the life of the holy community following the text of Holy Scripture. It consists of two movements. First it gets us into the sanctuary, the place of adoration and attention, listening and receiving and believing before God. There is a lot involved, all the parts of our lives ordered to all aspects of the revelation of God in Jesus.

Then it gets us out of the sanctuary into the world into places of obeying and loving, ordering our lives as living sacrifices in the world to the glory of God. There is a lot involved, all the parts of our lives out on the street participating in the work of salvation.

This is the kind of thing that St. John does so impressively in the Apocalypse: presents us with everything there is, the world and our experience in it, Christ and all his angels, the Devil and all his angels, heaven and hell, salvation and damnation, congregations and empires, war and peace — everything visible and invisible — and makes an act of worship out of it. He then shows how everything in that world of worship spills into the world. There are no nonparticipants. No one is standing around watching.

What St. John does so masterfully in the Apocalypse, we continue to do liturgically in the holy community under the shaping of the Holy Spirit as it is given textuality in Holy Scripture.

Liturgy preserves and presents the Holy Scriptures in the context of the worshipping and obeying community of Christians who are at the center of everything God has done, is doing, and will do. The liturgy won't let us go off alone with our Bibles, or self-select a few friends for Bible study and let it go at that.

The liturgical practice of the church presents us with the Holy Scriptures read and listened to and believed in the context of everything that is:

Architecture is part of it — the use of stone and timber and glass.

Color — purples and greens, reds and whites — is part of it.

Song is part of it — our hymns and anthems, our organs and guitars, our clarinets and drums.

Ancestors are part of it — the saints and scholars who enrich our preaching and prayers.

Prayer is part of it — prayers individual and corporate, voicing our deeply personal response to God and the call of God to praise and witness and mission.

Neighbors are part of it — these men and women and children with such different tastes and temperaments from us, many of whom we don't like very much.

And time. Liturgy gathers the holy community as it reads the Holy Scriptures into the sweeping tidal rhythms of the church year in which the story of Jesus and the Christian makes its rounds century after century, the large and easy interior rhythms of a year that moves from birth, life, death, resurrection, on to spirit, obedience, faith, and blessing. Without liturgy we lose the rhythms and end up tangled in the jerky, ill-timed, and insensitive interruptions of public-relations campaigns, school openings and closings, sales days, tax deadlines, inventories, and elections. Advent is buried under "shopping days before Christmas." The joyful disciplines of Lent are exchanged for the anxious penitentials of filling out income tax forms. Liturgy keeps us in touch with the story as it defines and shapes our beginnings and ends, our living and dying, our rebirths and blessing in this Holy Spirit, text-formed community, visible and invisible.

When Holy Scripture is embraced liturgically, we become aware that a lot is going on all at once, a lot of different people are doing a lot of different things. The community is on its feet, at work for God, listening and responding to the Holy Scriptures. The holy community, in the process of being formed by the Holy Scriptures, is watching/listening to God's revelation taking shape before and in them as they follow Jesus, each person playing his or her part in the Spirit.

It is useful to reflect that the word "liturgy" did not originate in church or worship settings. In the Greek world it referred to public service, what a citizen did for the community. As the church used the word in relation to worship, it kept this "public service" quality — working for the community on behalf of or following orders from God. As we worship God, revealed personally as Father, Son, and Holy Spirit in our Holy Scriptures, we are not doing something apart from or away from the non-Scripture-reading world; we do it *for* the world — bringing all creation and all history before God, presenting our bodies and all the beauties and needs of humankind before God in praise and intercession, penetrating and serving the world for whom Christ died in the strong name of the Trinity.

Liturgy puts us to work along with all the others who have been and are being put to work in the world by and with Jesus, following our spirituality-forming text. Liturgy keeps us in touch with all the action that has been and is being generated by the Spirit as given witness in the biblical text. Liturgy prevents the narrative form of Scripture from being reduced to private, individualized consumption.

Understood this way "liturgical" has little to do with choreography in the chancel or an aesthetics of the sublime. It is obedient, participatory listening to Holy Scripture in the company of the holy community through time (our two thousand years of responding to this text) and in space (our friends in Christ all over the world). High-church Anglicans, revivalistic Baptists, hands-in-the-air praising charismatics, and Quakers sitting in a bare room in silence are all required to read and live this text liturgically, participating in the holy community's reading of Holy Scripture. There is nothing "churchy" or elitist about it; it is a vast and dramatic "story-ing," making sure that we are taking our place in the story and letting everyone else have their parts in the story also, making sure that we don't leave anything or anyone out of the story. Without sufficient liturgical support and structure we are very apt to edit the story down to fit our individual tastes and predispositions.

Virtuoso Spirituality

Frances Young uses the extended analogy of music and its performance to provide a way of understanding the interrelated complexities of reading and living the Holy Scriptures, what John experienced as eating the book. Her book *Virtuoso Theology* searches out what she names as "the complex challenges involved in seeking authenticity in performance."[9] It is of the very nature of music that it is to be performed. Can music that is not performed be called "music"? Performance, though, does not consist in accurately reproducing the notes in the score as written by the composer, although it includes this. Everyone recognizes the difference between an accurate but wooden performance of, say, Mozart's Violin Concerto No. 1, and a virtuoso performance by Yitzak Perlman. Perlman's performance is not distinguished merely by his technical skill in reproducing what Mozart composed; he wondrously enters into and conveys the spirit and energy — the "life" — of the score. Significantly, he adds nothing to the score, neither "jot nor tittle." Even though he might reasonably claim that, with access to the interrelated psychologies of music and sexuality, he understands Mozart much better than Mozart understood himself, he restrains himself; he does not interpolate.

One of the continuous surprises of musical and dramatic performance is the sense of fresh spontaneity that comes in the performance: faithful attention to the text does not result in slavish efface-

9. Frances Young, *Virtuoso Theology* (Cleveland: Pilgrim, 1993), p. 21.

ment of personality; rather, it releases what is inherent in the text itself as the artist performs; "music has to be 'realized' through performance and interpretation."[10]

Likewise Holy Scripture. The two analogies, performing the music and eating the book, work admirably together. The complexity of the performance analogy supplements the earthiness of the eating analogy (and vice versa) in directing the holy community to enter the world of Holy Scripture formationally.

But if we are "unscripted," Alasdair MacIntyre's word in this context,[11] we spend our lives as anxious stutterers in both our words and actions. But when we do this rightly — performing the score, eating the book, embracing the holy community that internalizes this text — we are released into freedom: "I will run in the way of thy commandments when thou enlargest my understanding" (Ps. 119:32).

10. Young, *Virtuoso Theology*, p. 22. The "performance" analogy has also been used effectively by Nicholas Lash, "Performing the Scriptures," in *Theology on the Way to Emmaus* (London: SCM, 1986); and Brian Jenner, "Music to the Sinner's Ear?" *Epworth Review* 16 (1989): 35-38.

11. Alasdair MacIntyre, *After Virtue* (Notre Dame: University of Notre Dame Press, 1981), p. 216.

II

LECTIO DIVINA

"How do you read?"

LUKE 10:26

"You can't hear God speak to someone else, you can hear him only if you are being addressed."

LUDWIG WITTGENSTEIN

CHAPTER 6

Caveat Lector

Lectio divina is a way of reading the Scriptures that is congruent with the way the Scriptures serve the Christian community as a witness to God's revelation of himself to us. It is the wise guidance developed through the centuries of devout Bible reading to discipline us, the readers of Scripture, into appropriate ways of understanding and receiving this text so that it is formative for the way we live our lives, not merely making an impression on our minds or feelings. It intends the reading of Scripture to be a permeation of our lives by the revelation of God.

Reading the Bible, if we do not do it rightly, can get us into a lot of trouble. The Christian community is as concerned with *how* we read the Bible as *that* we read it. It is not sufficient to place a Bible in a person's hands with the command, "Read it." That is quite as foolish as putting a set of car keys in an adolescent's hands, giving him a Honda, and saying, "Drive it." And just as dangerous. The danger is that in having our hands on a piece of technology, we will use it ignorantly, endangering our lives and the lives of those around us; or that, intoxicated with the power that the technology gives us, we will use it ruthlessly and violently.

For print is technology. We pick up a Bible and find that we have God's word in our hands, *our hands*. We can now handle it. It is easy enough to suppose that we are in control of it, that we can use it, that we are in charge of applying it wherever, whenever, and to whomever we wish without regard to appropriateness or conditions.

There is more to the Honda than the technology of mechanics. And there is more to the Bible than the technology of print. Surrounding the machine technology of the Honda there is a world of gravity and inertia, values and velocity, surfaces and obstructions, Chevrolets and Fords, traffic regulations and the highway patrol, other drivers whether drunk or sober, snow and ice and rain. There is far more to driving a car than turning a key in the ignition and stepping on the accelerator. Those who don't know that are soon dead or maimed.

And those who don't know the conditions implicit in the technology of the Bible are likewise dangerous to themselves and others. And so, as we hand out Bibles and urge people to read them, it is imperative that we also say, *caveat lector*, let the reader beware.

Men and women shopping in the market for vegetables and meat, for carpets and skirts, for horses and automobiles have historically been warned by their experienced parents and grandparents, *caveat emptor*, let the buyer beware. The market is not always what it seems. More is going on here than a simple exchange of goods. Sellers and buyers seldom share identical values and goals. Sellers are not well known for looking out for the best interests of buyers. *Caveat emptor*, let the buyer beware.

And let the reader beware. Just having print on the page and knowing how to distinguish nouns from verbs is not enough. I might own a morocco leather Bible, having paid fifty dollars for it, but I don't own the word of God to do with what I want; *God* is sovereign. The word of God is not my possession. The words printed on the pages of my Bible give witness to the living and active revelation of the God of creation and salvation, the God of love who became the Word made flesh in Jesus, and I had better not forget it. If in my Bible reading I lose touch with this livingness, if I fail to listen to this living Jesus, submit to this sovereignty, and respond to this love, I become arrogant in my knowing and impersonal in my behavior. An enormous amount of damage is done in the name of Christian living by bad Bible reading. *Caveat lector*, let the reader beware.

A question Jesus posed to the religion scholar (the *nomikos*) who met him one day on the road to Jerusalem and commenced to grill him focuses our attention in these matters: "How do you read?" (*pōs anaginōskeis*, Luke 10:26). *How* do you read this, not *what* have you just read?[1]

Jesus' question is his answer to the scholar's question. The scholar had just asked Jesus, "What must I do to inherit eternal life?" It appears on the surface to be a perfectly legitimate question. But Luke, who is telling us this story, was on to something that was just below the surface. He lets us know that the religion scholar's question was hostile. The scholar wasn't asking for information or for counsel on how to live appropriately before God; his question was put forward "to test Jesus" (*ekpeiradzōn*). He wanted to provoke Jesus, or argue with him, or trip him up in some way or other. The same verb (*ekpeiradzein*) was used earlier by Luke to designate what the Devil was up to with Jesus in the wilderness (Luke 4:12), and in its noun form it is what Jesus a few lines later in the story (11:4) will teach us to pray for protection against (*peirasmon*). We don't know precisely what was behind the religion scholar's question, but it is clear enough that it wasn't an innocent question. The man was out to "get" Jesus somehow or other and use Scripture to do it.

Jesus' question evokes a correct answer from the scholar, an accurate and appropriate quotation of the double love command drawn from Deuteronomy 6:5 and Leviticus 19:18. Jesus readily gives his imprimatur to the man — "you have given the right answer." Jesus had himself, after all, combined the two texts in a conversation reported by Mark and Matthew in which a religion scholar had similarly questioned him (Matt. 22:34-40; Mark 12:28-31). There was nothing wrong with the scholar's knowledge of Scripture. But there was something terribly wrong in the way he read it, the *how* of his reading. This becomes evident when the scholar quibbles, "wanting to justify himself." He asks, "And who is my neighbor?"

---

1. AV, RSV, and NIV all translate Luke's *pōs* literally as "how." The NRSV translation, "what," is unfortunate, obscuring an essential detail.

Why does the scholar ask for a definition? Clearly, because he needs to defend himself against responding to the text personally. Defining "neighbor" depersonalizes the neighbor, turns him or her into an object, a thing over which he can take control, do with whatever he wants. But it also depersonalizes the scriptural text. He wants to talk *about* the text, treat the text as a thing, dissect it, analyze it, discuss it — endlessly. But Jesus won't play that game. The scholar has just quoted words of Holy Scripture that witness to the living word of God. They are words to be listened to, submitted to, obeyed, *lived*. So instead of inviting the scholar to join him in a Bible study of Deuteronomy and Leviticus under the shade of a nearby oak tree, Jesus tells him a story, one of his most famous, the Good Samaritan story, concluding, as he had begun, with a question, "Which of these three, do you think, proved neighbor to the man . . . ?" The scholar is impaled by the question: the words of Scripture can no longer be handled by means of definition, "who is my neighbor?" The text insists on participation, "will you be a neighbor?" *Jesus* insists on participation. Jesus dismisses the scholar with a command, "Go and do. . . ." Live what you read. We read the Bible in order to live the word of God.

Lectio *divina* cultivates this personal, participatory attentiveness and thus trains us in the discipline of reading Scripture rightly. At every turn of the page it poses Jesus' question to us: "*How* do you read?"

Here is another *caveat* that requires posting: words written are dead words. There is no life in them: "the letter kills" (2 Cor. 3:6 NRSV). Reading, as such, even if it is reading the Bible (maybe especially if it is reading the Bible) is nothing more than a devout stroll through a cemetery taking rubbings of inscriptions from ancient tombstones and grave markers. All those words written, coffined in the books of the world, buried in the libraries of the world, are dead words. But it is not as bad as that; these are not just dead words but dead words awaiting resurrection: for "the Spirit gives life" (2 Cor. 3:6).

Lectio *divina* finds itself in the company of the Galilean women who "prepared spices and ointments" (Luke 23:56) after the crucifixion, planning on the next day to honor and give dignity to the recently deceased body of Jesus, the Word made flesh. These women, when they arrive at the tomb, do not find what they expected ("they did not find the body") but learn to their total surprise from an angel that they are dealing not with a dead Jesus but with a live Jesus ("Why do you seek the living among the dead?"). Not the Word of God dead and buried in a tomb, but the Word of God resurrection-alive in the neighborhood. They leave their spices and ointments at the tomb — they have no use for them; Jesus has no use for them. They are on their way, ready to meet and follow and listen to the Word alive, Jesus. Ready to join the company of the Emmaus pilgrims, listening to Jesus interpret "to them in all the scriptures the things concerning himself" (Luke 24:27).

Lectio divina is the deliberate and intentional practice of making the transition from a kind of reading that treats and handles, however reverently, Jesus dead to a way of reading that frequents the company of friends who are listening to, accompanying, and following Jesus alive.

One more *caveat lector*. Words written are radically removed from their originating context, which is the living voice. And there is far more involved in listening to a living voice than reading a written word. Words are spoken and heard before they are written and read. Language was spoken long, long before it was written. There are still communities that get along satisfactorily without a written language, but none that survive without speech. Words are first of all an oral/aural phenomenon. Most of the words in our Scriptures were not formed first in writing — they were spoken and heard. The so-called "biblical world" that we orient ourselves in by means of the Bible for the most part did not have a Bible to read. Many, many generations of our biblical ancestors believed and obeyed and worshipped God without a script. They had the word of God, true enough, but they heard it, they listened to it. The word of God came by means of a voice.[2] We need to be repeatedly re-

2. James Barr is vigorous in making this point, emphasizing the necessity of personally recognizing the basic orality of what is given to us in Scripture: "In what we call 'biblical times', or in much of them, there was as yet no Bible. The men of the Bible

minded of this lest we lose touch with the basic orality of God's word in our lives.

But it is not only the timbre and tone and rhythm of the personal speaking voice that disappears in the act of writing, it is also the entire complex intricacy of other voices buzzing in the background, children interrupting with demands and questions, thrushes singing, the sound of the rain on the roof, the fragrance of juniper burning in the fireplace, the bouquet of the wine and texture of the bread that accompanies conversation at the table. The moment a word or a sentence is written it is detached from its origins and lands on the page as isolated as an artifact in a museum or a specimen in the laboratory. In the museum and laboratory we usually count this removal from context an advantage: we can now label it, define its properties, pick it up, turn it this way and that in the light, weigh it, measure it, write about it. With rocks and bones, pottery shards and computer chips, blood and urine specimens — things — the less context we have, the more exact we can be. Context contaminates and interferes with precision. But not so with words. So *caveat lector.*

Words are inherently ambiguous. They are never exact: the character of the person speaking influences how we interpret them; the attentiveness or intelligence of the listener affects how they are understood; place and weather and circumstances all play a part in both the speaking and the hearing. The more we are "in context" when language is used, the more likely we are to get it. Barely suppressed irritation and impatient finger tapping, hesitations and silences, gestures and grins and grimaces are all part of it. But the moment the words are written, all of that, or at least most of it, is gone. Even when the context is described, the complex simultaneity of interplay and intricacy is lost. Which means that when a word is written it is reduced. A word written is less than a word spoken — and sometimes not even the same thing

---

were, as we now see it, engaged in the process out of which our Bible in the end would emerge, but they themselves had no Bible ... the time of the Bible was a time when the Bible was not yet there. ..." See his *Holy Scripture* (Philadelphia: Westminster, 1983), pp. 1-2.

at all. Walter Ong has provided us with a careful assessment of the immense difference involved in hearing a word and reading a word.

> We are the most abject prisoners of the literate culture in which we
> have matured. Even with the greatest effort, contemporary man
> finds it exceedingly difficult, and in many instances quite impossible, to sense what the spoken word actually is. He feels it as a modification of something which normally is or ought to be written.[3]

Which, of course, is why many of us prefer words written to words spoken. It is simpler, we are more in control, we don't have to deal with the complexities of difficult, neurotic, or insufferably boring people. If we don't like what we are reading we can shut the book and pick up another — or go shopping, or take a walk, or spend an hour or so in the garden.

But *caveat lector:* we do not read the Bible in order to reduce our lives to what is convenient to us or manageable by us — we want to get in on the great invisibles of the Trinity, the soaring adorations of the angels, the quirky cragginess of the prophets, and . . . Jesus.

Jesus' lead-off parable in each of the first three Gospels emphasizes that the centrality of the word of God in our lives is not about reading but about listening: "Let anyone with ears to hear listen!" (cf. Matt. 13:3-9; Mark 4:3-9; Luke 8:5-8) The punch line of each of John of Patmos's sermons to his seven churches is similar: "Let anyone who has an ear listen to what the Spirit is saying to the churches" (Rev. 2:7, 11, 17, 29; 3:6, 13, 22 NRSV). Listening is what we do when someone speaks to us; reading is what we do when someone writes to us. Speaking comes first. Writing is derivative from speaking. And if we are to get the full force of the word, God's word, we need to recover its atmosphere of spokenness.

Some years ago I was leading a youth group on a summer camping expedition. The director of the camp had purchased at bargain

3. Walter Ong, S.J., *The Presence of the Word* (New Haven: Yale University Press, 1967), p. 19.

prices a vast quantity of dehydrated foods from an army surplus out-let. For one particular evening meal to be cooked on the trail I selected pork chops from the pantry, paper thin dehydrated pork chops, plenty of pork chops for ravenous fourteen-year-old boys, but weighing only a few ounces. The directions instructed us to soak them in a bucket of water for one hour, which we did. We watched in amazement as they took on water and were transformed in the bucket into large, juicy pork chops. A great conclusion to a strenuous day on the trail was an-ticipated. We could hardly wait. By this time we had a fire of hot coals ready. We placed six pork chops in a large skillet and propped it over the coals. As soon as the heat penetrated the skillet, the chops virtually disappeared — in two minutes the water was gone and we were left with the paper thin slices of pig that we had started out with.

There is a sense in which the Scriptures are the word of God de-hydrated, with all the originating context removed — living voices, city sounds, camels carrying spices from Seba and gold from Ophir snorting down in the bazaar, fragrance from lentil stew simmering in the kitchen — all now reduced to marks on thin onion-skin paper. We make an effort at rehydrating them; we take these Scriptures and spend an hour or so in Bible study with friends or alone in prayerful reading. But five minutes later, on our way to work, plunged into the tasks of the day for which they had seemed to promise sustenance, there's not much left of them — only ink on india paper. We find that we are left with the words of the Bible but without the world of the Bi-ble. Not that there is anything wrong with the words as such, it is just that without the biblical world — the intertwined stories, the echoing poetry and prayers, Isaiah's artful thunder and John's extravagant vi-sions — the words, like those seed words in Jesus' parable that land on pavement or in gravel or among weeds, haven't take root in our lives.

Lectio divina is the strenuous effort that the Christian community gives (Austin Farrer's "formidable discipline"!) to rehydrating the Scriptures so that they are capable of holding their own original force and shape in the heat of the day, maintaining their context long enough to get fused with or assimilated into our context, the world we inhabit, the clamor of voices in the daily weather and work in which we live. But it takes more than an hour in the bucket to accomplish what is needed. *Lectio divina* is a way of life that develops "according to the Scriptures." It is not just a skill that we exercise when we have a Bible open before us but a life congruent with the Word made flesh to which the Scriptures give witness. The Letter to the Hebrews tells us that the word of God originated when "long ago God *spoke* to our ancestors in many and various ways by the prophets, but in these last days he has *spoken* to us by a Son. . . . Therefore we must pay greater attention to what we have *heard* . . ." (Heb. 1:1-2; 2:1; emphasis added). These are spoken words delivered to us by "so great a cloud of witnesses" (Heb. 12:1) and now written in our Holy Scriptures. It is the task of *lectio divina* to get those words heard and listened to, words written in ink now rewritten in blood.

CHAPTER 7

"Ears Thou Hast Dug for Me"

So, *lectio divina.*

A way of reading that guards against depersonalizing the text into an affair of questions and answers, definitions and dogmas. A way of reading that prevents us from turning Scripture on its head and using it to justify ourselves like that pathetic religion scholar was trying to do with Jesus. A way of reading that abandons the attempt to take control of the text as if it were helpless without our help. A way of reading that joins the company of Galilean women at the tomb as they abandon the spices and ointments with which they were going to take care of the Word made flesh, the Jesus they expected to find wrapped in grave clothes, and embrace the resurrection of that same Word and all the words brought to life in him. A way of reading that intends the fusion of the entire biblical story and my story. A way of reading that refuses to be reduced to *just* reading but intends the living of the text, listening and responding to the voices of that "so great a cloud of witnesses" telling their stories, singing their songs, preaching their sermons, praying their prayers, asking their questions, having their children, burying their dead, following Jesus.

Lectio divina provides us with a discipline, developed and handed down by our ancestors, for recovering the context, restoring the intricate web of relationships to which the Scriptures give witness but that are so easily lost or obscured in the act of writing.

It is time to deal with the details. What exactly is involved? How do we go about this?

Lectio divina comprises four elements: *lectio* (we read the text), *meditatio* (we meditate the text), *oratio* (we pray the text), and *contemplatio* (we live the text). But naming the four elements must be accompanied by a practiced awareness that their relationship is not sequential. Reading *(lectio)* is a linear act, but spiritual *(divina)* reading is not — any of the elements may be at the fore at any one time. There is a certain natural progression from one to another, but after separating them in order to understand them we find that in actual practice they are not four discrete items that we engage in one after another in stair-step fashion. Rather than linear the process is more like a looping spiral in which all four elements are repeated, but in various sequences and configurations. What we are after is *noticing,* seeing the interplay — elements not marching in precise formation but one calling forth another and then receding to give place to another, none in isolation from the others but thrown together in a kind of playful folk dance. They are like sodium and chlorine, very dangerous, lethal even, in isolation but as a compound, sodium chloride, table salt, bringing life to otherwise bland foods. Each of the elements must be taken seriously; none of the elements may be eliminated; none of the elements can be practiced in isolation from the others. In the actual practice of *lectio divina* the four elements fuse, interpenetrate. *Lectio divina* is a way of reading that becomes a way of living.[1]

I want to re-say what our Christian companions have been saying

---

1. This classic formulation of *lectio divina*, preceded by a thousand years of practices intended to shape reading into living, was by a European monk, Guigo the Second in the twelfth century. Among his many elaborations of the exercise this one is characteristic: "Reading, as it were, puts the solid food into our mouths, meditation chews it and breaks it down, prayer obtains the flavour of it and contemplation is the very sweetness which makes us glad and refreshes us." Quoted and commented on by Simon Tugwell, O.P., *Ways of Imperfection* (Springfield, Ill.: Templegate, 1985), p. 94.

in a variety of ways for two millennia, with a few modifications that fit them into our present context.

An arresting phrase in Psalm 40:6 serves admirably as a metaphor for *lectio divina*: *'aznayim karitha li*, literally, "ears thou hast dug for me." Translators routinely but timidly paraphrase: "thou hast given me an open ear" (RSV); "my ears you have pierced" (NIV); "mine ears thou hast opened" (KJV). But the psalms poet was bold to imagine God swinging a pickax, digging ears in our granite blockheads so that we can hear, really hear, what he speaks to us.

The primary organ for receiving God's revelation is not the eye that sees but the ear that hears — which means that all of our reading of Scripture must develop into a hearing of the word of God.

Print technology — a wonderful thing, in itself — has put millions and millions of Bibles in our hands, but unless these Bibles are embedded in the context of a personally speaking God and a prayerfully listening community, we who handle these Bibles are at special risk. If we reduce the Bible to a tool to be used, the tool builds up calluses on our hearts.

Lectio

Reading may seem to be the first thing, but it is not. Reading is always preceded by hearing and speaking. Language is essentially oral. We learn our language not from a book, not from a person writing words, but from a person speaking them. The written word has the potential to resurrect the speaking voice and listening ear, but it does not insist upon it. The word can just sit there on the page and be analyzed or admired or ignored. Just because we have read it doesn't mean we have heard it.

The written word is also clearer than the spoken word. Language, as we speak and hear it, is very ambiguous. We miss a lot, we misunderstand a lot. No matter how logically and plainly things are said, the listener quite often doesn't get it right. Conversely, no matter how attentive and knowledgeable the listener, the speaker often doesn't say it right. We proceed, as T. S. Eliot once put it, by "hints followed by guesses."[2] Just because we have looked up the word in our dictionary and have carefully cross-referenced it doesn't guarantee that we have listened to and heard the voice of the living God.

I sometimes marvel that God chose to risk his revelation in the ambiguities of language. If he had wanted to make sure that the truth was absolutely clear, without any possibility of misunderstanding, he should have revealed his truth by means of mathematics. Mathematics is the most precise, unambiguous language that we have. But then, of course, you can't say "I love you" in algebra.

So it is important to not assume too much. It is important to listen to the counsel of our Christian brothers or sisters, who place an open Bible before us and tell us, "Read. Read only what is here, but also be sure that you read it the *way* that it is here." *Lectio.*

The place to begin, though, is not, as is often supposed, with a grammar and a dictionary. The fixity of the words on paper, removed from the nuances and ambiguities of the living voice, gives an illusion of preciseness and seems to invite a matching preciseness in the reader. We do better to begin with a consideration of metaphor, the most distinctive feature of language as we use it and a feature that is likewise prominent in Scripture. If we don't understand how metaphor works we will misunderstand most of what we read in the Bible. No matter how carefully we parse our Hebrew and Greek sentences, no matter how precisely we use our dictionaries and trace our etymologies, no matter how exactly we define the words on the page, if we do not appreciate the way a metaphor works we will never comprehend the meaning of the text.

Despite the frequency and prominence of metaphor in language, understanding its dynamics is not as easy as we might suppose, particularly when we come upon metaphor as readers instead of hearers, for

2. T. S. Eliot, "The Dry Salvages," *The Complete Poems and Plays* (New York: Harcourt, Brace, and Co., 1985), p. 136.

the word on the page gives the impression of being literal, composed as it is of letters fixed on the page in indelible ink. And of being unchanging — if we return to a page that we left off reading three days ago and re-read it, it is exactly the same as when we left it. That cannot be said of a voiced conversation.

The difficulty is compounded for most Bible readers because there is the assumption that what we are reading is the "word of God," which means that it absolutely must be taken seriously. But "seriously" in our present-day reading culture very often means literally. Science provides the standard by which we judge truth. Truth is what can be verified under laboratory conditions. Truth is what is empirically true — with things it is what we can test and probe, measure and weigh; with language it is what can survive strenuous logical analysis. It is what we often refer to as "literal."

Metaphor is a form of language that cannot pass such logical scrutiny, cannot make it through the laboratory tests. Unfortunately (or fortunately, as it turns out) the Bible is chock full of metaphor, which means that if we assume that "literal" is the only means to "serious" we are going to be in trouble much of the time. For a metaphor is literally a lie.

A metaphor states as true something that is literally not true. For instance, "God is a rock," a frequent Hebrew assertion about God ("The LORD is my rock. . . . [W]ho is a rock, except our God?" Ps. 18:2, 31). If we take the sentence literally, instead of going to church on Sunday mornings to worship we will visit the local stone quarry and shop for a god rock that we can erect in our backyard. The alternative is to dismiss the sentence as meaningless, which would leave us with a Bible with every other sentence or so deleted, including some of our most prized: the Lord is my shepherd (Ps. 23:1); the Lord is a warrior (Exod. 15:3); I am a rose of Sharon (Song 2:1); I am the true vine (John 15:1).

Sandra Schneiders expertly characterizes metaphor as language that "contains an 'is' and an 'is not,' held in irresolvable tension."[3] The

---

3. Sandra M. Schneiders, *The Revelatory Text* (San Francisco: HarperSanFrancisco, 1991), p. 29.

tension is inherently uncomfortable and administers a kind of shock treatment to the mind, stimulating it to a deeper involvement than what can be accounted for by a literal surface reading. If we suppress the "is" we kill the metaphor and end up with a mummified corpse of its meaning. If we suppress the "is not" we literalize the metaphor and end up with a junkyard of wrecked and rusted-out words.

The metaphor treated literally is simply absurd. But if we let it have its way with us, it pushes us to clarity at a different level. Take, for instance, the metaphors piled up in Psalm 114:

> The sea looked and fled,
> > Jordan turned back.
> The mountains skipped like rams,
> > the hills like lambs. (vv. 3-4)

It doesn't take us long to realize that this is an account of the exodus: "The sea looked and fled." In the sober language of prose, this is the story of Israel. Fleeing from the Egyptians and then blocked at the waters of the Red Sea, the people walked through on dry land after Moses struck the waters with his staff and the waters parted. God provided a way of escape. "Jordan turned back" remembers Israel's being prevented from entering the Promised Land at the conclusion of her forty years' wilderness trek by the formidable Jordan River. Then Joshua struck the waters with his staff, the river parted, and the people marched through and began their conquest of the land. God provided a way of victory. In the prose of the book of Exodus, "the mountains skipped like rams, the hills like lambs" is the story of the long wait of the people at the base of Sinai in awe before the volcanic-rumbling and earthquake-shaken mountain while Moses was on the heights receiving the law.

So, why not say it plainly? Tell it to us straight? Denise Levertov in her poem "Poetics of Faith" tells us why:

> "Straight to the point"
> > can ricochet,
> > > unconvincing,

circumlocution, analogy,
    parables, ambiguities, provide
        context, stepping-stones.[4]

For one thing, God's action and presence among us is so beyond our comprehension that sober description and accurate definition are no longer functional. The levels of reality here are so beyond us that they compel extravagance of language. But the language, though extravagant, is not exaggerated. All language, but especially language that deals with transcendence, with God, is inadequate and falls short. The metaphor of the Red Sea as a fleeing jackal, the Jordan as a cowardly sentinel forsaking his post, the transformation of Sinai into frolicking rams and lambs is not, of course, a journalistic account of what happened, but neither is it the fabrication of an unhinged imagination. It is a writer of God's revelation giving witness to salvation. The somersaulting of what everyone had assumed to be the limitations of reality (Red Sea and Jordan River) and the unexpected outpouring of energy from a huge, dead, granite outcropping in the dead desert (Sinai) called for metaphor.

This is an instance of what poet Wallace Stevens, himself a master of metaphor, called "a motive for metaphor."[5] By means of metaphor we see far more than discrete *things*, we perceive everything in dynamic tension and relationship with everything else. The raw stuff of the world is not matter but energy. How do we express this interconnected vitality? We use metaphor.

A metaphor is a word that bears a meaning beyond its naming function; the "beyond" extends and brightens our comprehension rather than confusing it. Just as the language of ecology demonstrates the interconnectedness of all *things* (air, water, soil, persons, birds, and so forth), the language of metaphor demonstrates the interconnected-

---

4. Denise Levertov, *The Stream and the Sapphire* (New York: New Directions, 1997), p. 31.

5. Northrop Frye quotes and discusses Stevens in *The Educated Imagination* (Bloomington: Indiana University Press, 1964), pp. 30-32.

ness of all *words*. The historical word (exodus), the geological word (hills), and the animal word (ram) all have to do with every other word.

Meanings interconnect. Nothing can be understood in isolation, pinned down under a microscope; no *word* can be understood by merely locating it in a dictionary. From the moment we speak, we are drawn into the total web of all language that has ever been spoken. One word draws us into surprising relationships with another, and then another, and then another. And that is why metaphor holds such a prominent place in Scripture, in which everything is in movement, finding its place in relation to the word that God speaks.

Wendell Berry says this well: "The earth is not dead like the concept of property, but is as vividly and intricately alive as a man or a woman and . . . there is a delicate interdependence between its life and our own."[6] And so the metaphorical statement "the mountains skip like rams" is not mere illustration to portray the exuberance of the Sinai revelation; it is a penetrating realization that the earth itself responds to and participates in that revelation. Paul used a different, though just as striking, metaphor for the action: "We know that the whole creation has been groaning in travail together until now; and not only the creation, but we ourselves" (Rom. 8:22-23). Metaphor does not explain; it does not define; it draws us away from being outsiders into being insiders, involved with all reality spoken into being by God's word.

Language is debased when it uses metaphor as decoration to cover scrawny thoughts, putting lace cuffs on bare-wristed prose. In actual fact, metaphorical language is not what we learn to use after we have mastered the rudiments of plain speech, it is prior to descriptive language — infants and poets are our exemplars.

Metaphor sends out tentacles of connectedness. As we find ourselves in the tumble and tangle of metaphors in Scripture we realize that we are not schoolboys and schoolgirls reading about God, gathering information or "doctrine" that we can study and use; we are resi-

---

6. Wendell Berry, *A Continuous Harmony* (New York: Harcourt Brace Jovanovich, 1972), p. 12.

dents in a home interpenetrated by spirit — God's Spirit, my spirit, your spirit. The metaphor makes us part of what we know. Each word draws us closer to where words come from: the creative word that makes mountains and rams, hills and lambs, Israel and Judah, Jacob and Christ, me and you. The word, and most conspicuously the metaphor, signals transcendence and encounter with the One who speaks everything into being.

This is the kind of reading upon which Scripture, profligate as it is with metaphor, insists.

Meditatio

Plato, writing at the moment when a primarily oral culture was giving way to writing, made the astute observation that writing was going to debilitate memory. Ivan Illich characterizes him as "the first uneasy man of letters," for Plato observed how his students' reliance on silent, passive texts narrowed the stream of their remembrance, making it shallow and dull.[7] When words were primarily exchanged by means of voices and ears, language was living and kept alive in acts of speaking and listening. But the moment that words were written, memory was bound to atrophy — we would no longer have to remember what was said; we could look it up in a book. Books rob us of the right and pleasure of answering back. He made his observation by telling a story that we can now "look up" in his book, *Phaedrus*.[8]

Here's the story. In Egypt there was a god by the name of Thoth. He was the inventor of many things, but his proudest invention was the letters that make writing possible. One day he was more or less showing off, bragging of his accomplishment before King Thamus, telling him that this would make the Egyptians wiser and give them

7. Ivan Illich and Barry Sanders, *The Alphabetization of the Popular Mind* (New York: Vintage, 1988), p. 24.

8. "Phaedrus," in *The Dialogues of Plato*, trans. Benjamin Jowett (New York: Random House, 1937, first published 1892), vol. 1, pp. 277-82.

better memories. King Thamus would have none of it. He said that it would ruin their memories, that it would have much more to do with forgetting than remembering, that they would have the show of words without the reality. Plato has Socrates comment on the story by comparing writing to painting. The figures in the landscape of the painter have "an attitude of life and yet if you ask them a question they preserve a solemn silence." Similarly, with writing, "put a question and they give the same unvarying answer." Once the words have been "written down they are tumbled about anywhere among those who may or may not understand them, and know not to whom they should reply, to whom not: and, if they are maltreated or abused, they have no parent to protect them; and they cannot protect or defend themselves." Socrates, who, like Jesus, never wrote anything, prefers a "living word which has a soul . . . graven in the soul of the learner, which can defend itself, and knows when to speak and when to be silent."

Northrop Frye summarizes Plato's concern this way: "The ability to record has a lot more to do with forgetting than with remembering: with keeping the past in the past, instead of continuously recreating it in the present."[9]

Meditatio is the discipline we give to keeping the memory active in the act of reading. Meditation moves from looking at the *words* of the text to entering the *world* of the text. As we take this text into ourselves, we find that the text is taking us into itself. For the world of the text is far larger and more real than our minds and experience. The biblical text is a witness to God revealing himself. This revelation is not simply a series of random oracles that illuminate momentary obscurities or guide us through perplexing circumstances. This text is *God*-revealing: God creating, God saving, God blessing. The text has a context and the context is huge, massive, comprehensive. St. Paul is staggered by it: "O the depth of the riches and wisdom and knowledge of God! How unsearchable are his judgments and how inscrutable his ways!" (Rom. 11:33).

---

9. Northrop Frye, *The Great Code: The Bible and Literature* (New York: Harcourt Brace Jovanovich, 1982), p. 22.

This world of revelation is not only large, it is coherent — everything is connected as in a living organism. A living God is revealing himself, and so if we are going to get it at all we must enter the large livingness of it. Meditation rehearses this largeness, enters into what is there, re-membering all the aspects that have been dismembered in our disobedience, noticing the connections, realizing the congruences, picking up the echoes. There is always more to anything, any word or sentence, than meets the eye; meditation enters into the large backgrounds that are not immediately visible, that we overlooked the first time around.

Meditation is the aspect of spiritual reading that trains us to read Scripture as a connected, coherent whole, not a collection of inspired bits and pieces.

In pagan antiquity there was a popular story about a woman who uttered divine oracles. Her name was Sibyl, and she was a prophetess from the Greek village of Cumae. She is first mentioned by Heraclitus in 500 B.C. I've always imagined her as an old crone with unfocused eyes and wild hair, sitting at the entrance to a cave stirring a kettle of foul-smelling brew and muttering sacred wisdom in a syntax that is familiar to us from fortune cookies. She got something started in Cumae that continued: "sibyls" kept showing up in various times and places, making oracular pronouncements in throaty voices that men and women took as divine counsel. Later Jewish and Christian "sibyls" got in on the act. People started collecting the oracles and putting them in a book. The collections grew and by the fourth century A.D. there were fifteen books of Sibylline Oracles, some of which a considerable number of Christians took quite seriously.[10]

Sibyl and her imitators were a ready source for divine counsel, providing wisdom and direction to confused men and women. The usual process was to enter a cave where the sibyl was stationed and listen to her muttered sounds. At times shrines were built at these sites. The sounds were cryptic, often apparent gibberish, but it was inspired

10. J. Knox, "Sibylline Oracles," *Interpreter's Dictionary of the Bible* (New York: Abingdon, 1962), vol. 4, p. 343.

gibberish and therefore highly prized as wisdom — truth from the source of truth. The oracles were without context, guttural or wheezy fragments of sound from the gods. But that was the great attraction. The oracles were the word of god coming to you without syntax or context — you were free to supply those incidentals yourself.

What is surprising today is how many people treat the Bible as a collection of Sibylline Oracles, verses or phrases without context or connections. This is nothing less than astonishing. The Scriptures are the revelation of a personal, relational, incarnational God to actual communities of men and women with names in history. The witnesses to the revelation are real writers who do their writing and witnessing in the full light of day and with the confirmation of their worshipping communities. Everything is out in the open. This is no muttering in a dark Aegean cave but the Holy Spirit operating under an open sky, bringing about legible, coherent writing that has continuities from generation to generation, a narrative with plot and characters and scenery.

The practice of dividing the Bible into numbered chapters and verses has abetted this "sibylline complex." It gives the impression that the Bible is a collection of thousands of self-contained sentences and phrases that can be picked out or combined arbitrarily in order to discern our fortunes or fates. But Bible verses are not fortune cookies to be broken open at random. And the Bible is not an astrological chart to be impersonally manipulated for amusement or profit.

Meditation is the primary way in which we guard against the fragmentation of our Scripture reading into isolated oracles. Meditation enters into the coherent universe of God's revelation. Meditation is the prayerful employ of imagination in order to become friends with the text. It must not be confused with fancy or fantasy.

Meditation doesn't make things up. We are wedded to a historic faith and are rightly wary of the intrusion of human invention. But meditation is not intrusion, it is rumination — letting the images and stories of the entire revelation penetrate our understanding. By meditation we make ourselves at home and conversant with everyone in the story, entering the place where Moses and Elijah and Jesus converse together. Participation is necessary. Meditation is participation.

I like Warren Wiersbe's distinction between fancy and imagination: "Fancy wrote 'Mary had a little lamb' but inspired imagination wrote 'The Lord is my Shepherd.' Fancy creates a new world for you; imagination gives you insight into the old world."[11]

No text can be understood out of its entire context. The most "entire" context is Jesus. Every biblical text must be read in the living presence of Jesus. Every word of the scriptural text is a window or door leading us out of the tarpaper shacks of self into this great outdoors of God's revelation in sky and ocean, tree and flower, Isaiah and Mary, and, finally and completely, Jesus. Meditation discerns the connections and listens for the harmonies that come together in Jesus.

We meditate to become empathetic with the text. We move from being critical outsiders to becoming appreciative insiders. The text is no longer something to be looked at with cool and detached expertise but something to be entered into with the playful curiosity of a child.

G. K. Chesterton's fictional Father Brown shows us how it is done. Nearing the conclusion of his colorful career as a sleuth in priest's clothing, having solved many intricate and complex criminal cases, he is talking with some friends while sitting around a late-night fireplace in a friend's home in the mountains of Spain. One of the friends asks him the secret to his many successes in solving crimes. Blinking his big expressionless eyes behind the little round glasses, he blandly replies, "You see, it was I who killed all those people." Everyone gasps, staring with appalled astonishment at the timid, mousy priest. Then he goes on, "I had thought out exactly how a thing like that could be done, and in what style or state of mind a man could really do it. And when I was quite sure that I felt exactly like the murderer himself, of course I knew who he was."[12]

11. Warren Wiersbe, *Leadership Journal* (spring 1983): 23.
12. G. K. Chesterton, *The Father Brown Stories* (1929).

Oratio

There is more. There is prayer — *oratio*. "Bible searching and searching prayer go hand in hand. What we receive from God in the Book's message we return to Him with interest in prayer," writes P. T. Forsyth.[13] Spiritual reading requires a disciplined attention to exactly the way the text is written; it requires a meditative and receptive entering into the world of the text; and it requires response. We read and enter and before long we, in some surprise, say, "Oh, this has to do with *me!* God's word is addressed to me — I'm the one spoken to!" It is one thing to be listening to God speak to Moses on the austere crags of Mount Sinai or listening to Jesus preach the Beatitudes on a grassy Galilean hillside, thrilling to the truth, admiring the majesty. It's quite another thing entirely to realize that God is speaking to me bicycling in the rain down a country road in Kentucky. I'm speechless; or I stutter. How do I answer God? But answer I do, for the text requires it.

Prayer is language used in relation to God. It is the most universal of all languages, the *lingua franca* of the human heart. Prayer ranges from "sighs too deep for words" (Rom. 8:26) to petitions and thanksgivings composed in lyric poetry and stately prose to "psalms and hymns and spiritual songs" (Col. 3:16) to the silence of a person present to God in attentive adoration (Ps. 62:1).

The foundational presupposition of all prayer is that God reveals himself personally by means of language. The word of God is not placarded on a billboard, an impersonal notice posted to call our attention to something that God once said or did, while we are driving down the road to somewhere else. God creates the cosmos with words; he creates us with words; he calls to us, speaks to us, whispers to us using words. Then he gives us, his human creatures, the gift of language; we not only can hear and understand God as he speaks to us, we can speak to him — respond, answer, converse, argue, question. We can pray. God is the initiator and guarantor of language both ways, as God

---

13. P. T. Forsyth, *The Soul of Prayer* (London: Independent Press, 1916), p. 46.

speaks to us, as we speak to God. It is a wonder that God speaks to us; it is hardly less a wonder that God listens to us. The biblical revelation is equally insistent on both counts: the efficacy of God's language to us, the efficacy of our language to God. Our listening to God is an on-again, off-again affair; God always listens to us. The essential reality of prayer is that its source and character are entirely in God. We are most ourselves when we pray. But prayer is not a human-based activity. Psychology doesn't get us very far in either understanding or practicing prayer. Whether we are aware of it or not (and often we are not), it begins and ends and has its being in the company of the Trinity.

The Scriptures, read and prayed, are our primary and normative access to God as he reveals himself to us. The Scriptures are our listening post for learning the language of the soul, the ways God speaks to us; they also provide the vocabulary and grammar that are appropriate for us as we in our turn speak to God. Prayer detached from Scripture, from listening to God, disconnected from God's words to us, short-circuits the relational language that is prayer. Christians acquire this personal and relational practice of prayer primarily (although not exclusively) under the shaping influence of the Psalms and Jesus.

The Psalms are the preeminent witness to our praying participation as we read or listen to God's word. Athanasius caught their genius succinctly when he said, "Most scriptures speak *to* us; the Psalms speak *for* us." And oh, how they speak. They don't simply say, "Yes, God, I agree. Yes that's right, I couldn't have said it better myself." Or, "Yes, would you say that again so I can write it down and show it to my friends." No, they argue and complain, they lament and they praise, they deny and declaim, they thank and they sing. On one page they accuse God of betraying and abandoning them and on the next they turn cartwheels of hallelujahs. Sometimes we suppose that the proper posture of response to God as we read the Bible is to be curled up in a wingback chair before a cozy fire, docile and well-mannered. Some of us are taught to think that reading the Bible means sitting in God's classroom and that prayer is politely raising our hand when we have a question about what he is teaching us in his Deuteronomy lecture. The Psalms, our prayer text within the biblical text, show us something quite different: prayer is *engaging* God, an engaging that is seldom accomplished by a murmured greeting and a conventional handshake. The engagement, at least in its initial stages, is more like a quarrel than a greeting, more like a wrestling match than a warm embrace.[14]

And how could it be otherwise? This world, this reality, revealed by God speaking to us, is not the kind of world to which we are accustomed. It is not a neat and tidy world in which we are in control — there is mystery everywhere that takes considerable getting used to, and until we do it scares us. It is not a predictable, cause-effect world in which we can plan our careers and secure our futures — there is miracle everywhere that upsets us no end, except for the occasions when the miracle is in our favor. It is not a dream world in which everything works out according to our adolescent expectations — there is suffering and poverty and abuse at which we cry out in pain and indignation, "You can't let this happen!" For most of us it takes years and years and years to exchange our dream world for the real world of grace and mercy, sacrifice and love, freedom and joy.

Using the Psalms as a school of prayer, praying these prayers we get a feel for what is appropriate to say as we bring our lives into attentive and worshipping response to God as he speaks to us. As we do this, the first thing we realize is that in prayer anything goes. Virtually everything human is appropriate as material for prayer: reflections and observations, fear and anger, guilt and sin, questions and doubts, needs and desires, praise and gratitude, suffering and death. Nothing human is excluded. The Psalms are an extended refutation that prayer is "being nice" before God. No — prayer is an offering of ourselves, just as we

---

14. "The working out of the biblical model for the understanding of God was not an intellectual process so much as a personal conflict, in which men struggled with their God, and with each other about their God. It was, in Old Testament terms, a *ribh* or dispute, a controversy to which the public attention is drawn so that men can learn from it. If there are distortions in the biblical picture of God, they belong not only to inadequate vision but to human resistance against God's truth and against insights seen by other men." James Barr, *The Bible in the Modern World* (London: SCM, 1973), p. 119.

are. The second thing we realize is that prayer is access to everything that God is for us: holiness, justice, mercy, forgiveness, sovereignty, blessing, vindication, salvation, love, majesty, glory. The Psalms are a detailed demonstration that prayer brings us into the welcoming presence of God as he generously offers himself, just as he is, to us.

Luther, in his preface to the German Psalter (1528), wrote,

> if you want to see the holy Christian Church painted in glowing colors and in a form which is really alive, and if you want this to be done in a miniature, you must get hold of the Psalter, and there you will have in your possession a fine, clear, pure mirror which will show you what Christianity really is; yea, you will find yourself in it and the true *gnothi seauton* ["know thyself"], and God himself and all his creatures, too.[15]

If the Psalms are our primary text for prayer, our answering speech to the word of God, then Jesus, the Word made flesh, is our primary teacher. Jesus is the divine/human personal center for a life of prayer. Jesus prays for us — "he always lives to make intercession for [us]" (Heb. 7:25). The verb is in the present tense. This is the most important thing to know about prayer, not that we should pray or how we should pray but that Jesus is right now praying for us (see also Heb. 4:16 and John 17). Jesus, the Word that made us (John 1:3; Col. 1:16), is also among us to teach us to direct our words personally to God. Mostly he did this by example; Luke cites nine instances: 5:16; 6:12; 9:18, 28; 11:1; 22:31, 41, 44; 24:30. But we have only a slim accounting of his actual prayers. Some are inarticulate (Mark 7:34; 8:12; John 11:33; Heb. 5:7). Some are quoted verbatim (Matt. 11:25; 26:39; 27:46; Luke 23:46; John 11:41; 12:27-28; 17:1-26).

The single instance in which Jesus instructed us in prayer was in response to the disciples' request, "Lord, teach us to pray . . ." (Luke 11:1). His answer, "When you pray, say . . . ," our so-called Lord's Prayer (Luke

15. Quoted by Artur Weiser, *The Psalms* (Philadelphia: Westminster, 1962), pp. 19-20.

11:2-4 and Matt. 6:9-13), is the church's primary text (backed up by the Psalms) for guiding Christians into a life of personal, honest, and mature prayer. The simplicity and brevity of Jesus' first (and only!) lesson in prayer is striking, a standing rebuke against all attempts to develop techniques of prayer or to discover the "secret" of prayer. Prayer as Jesus practiced and taught it was not a verbal tool for working on God, not an insider formula for getting our way with God.

Prayer is shaped by Jesus, in whose name we pray. Our knowledge, our needs, our feelings are taken seriously, but they are not foundational. God, revealed in the Scriptures that we read and meditate upon and in Jesus whom we address, gives both form and content to our prayers. In prayer we are most ourselves; it is the one act in which we can, *must*, be totally ourselves. But it is also the act in which we move beyond ourselves. In that "move beyond" we come to be formed and defined not by the sum total of our experiences but by the Father, Son, and Spirit to whom and by whom we pray.

God does not make speeches; he enters conversations and we are partners to the conversation. We enter the syntax, the grammar of the word of God. We are not the largest part. We do not supply the verbs and nouns. But we are without question in it. We provide a preposition here, a conjunction there, an occasional enclitic or proclitic, once in awhile an adverb or adjective. Often it's only a semicolon or comma, an exclamation point or question mark. But we are *part* of the syntax, not external to it. The text assumes that we are participants in what is written, not accidental drop-ins, not hit or miss bystanders, not an addendum or footnote. By its very nature language connects; it is dialogic; it creates conversation.[16] Prayer is our entrance into the grammar of revelation, the grammar of the word of God.

The world revealed by God's word is so much larger than our sin-

16. "We often assume that the problem of interpreting words is a matter of knowing what they mean and linking meanings together in some reasonable order in our minds. But it's not quite like that. The problem is to decide at any moment what our relation to the words should be, even when we know what they mean." Denis Donoghue, *Ferocious Alphabets* (Boston: Little, Brown, 1976), p. 14.

conditioned world that we can't be expected to grasp it all at once. The world revealed by God's word has so much more to it, in it, and behind it than our ego-centered world that we can't be expected to understand it all at once. But God is patient with us. That is why we *pray* what we read. Prayer is the way we work our way out of the comfortable but cramped world of self into the self-denying but spacious world of God. It's getting rid of self so that we can be all soul — God-aware, God-dimensioned.

Reality as God reveals it to us by his word in Jesus is strange and unexpected and disappointing. This is not the kind of world we would have created if we had been given the assignment; this is not the kind of salvation we would have arranged if we had been on the committee; this is not the system of rewards and punishments we would have legislated if we had had the vote. I love the audacious quip of Teresa of Avila when she was energetically engaged in reforming the Carmelite monasteries, traveling all over Spain by oxcart on bad roads. One day she was thrown from her cart into a muddy stream. She shook her fist at God, "God, if this is the way you treat your friends, no wonder you don't have many."[17]

That's right. The reality that God reveals to us in his word is very different, quite other — Other! — than anything we could ever have dreamed up. And thank goodness, for if we keep at this long enough, prayer by prayer, we find ourselves living in a reality that is far larger, far lovelier, far better. But it takes considerable getting used to. Prayer is the process of getting used to it, going from the small to the large, from control to mystery, from self to soul — to God.

It is not easy. It was not easy for Jesus those nights on the mountain, that night in Gethsemane, those hours on the cross. Nobody ever said it would be easy. God didn't say it would be easy. But it's the way things are — this is the way the world is, the way we are, the way God is. Do you want to live in the real world? This is it. God doesn't reveal it to us by his word only so that we can *know* about it, he continues the revelation in us as we pray and participate in it.

17. Teresa of Ávila, *A Life of Prayer*, abridged and edited by James M. Houston (Portland: Multnomah Press, 1983), p. xxvii.

The necessity for sturdy and ready responsiveness to the Spirit as we read the text is on display in a diary entry by Julian Green for October 6, 1941:

> The story of the manna gathered and set aside by the Hebrews is deeply significant. It so happened that the manna rotted when it was kept. And perhaps this means that all spiritual reading which is not consumed — by prayer and by works — ends by causing a sort of rotting inside us. You die with a head full of fine sayings and a perfectly empty heart.[18]

We are well warned: it is not enough to understand the Bible, or admire it. God has spoken; now it's our move. We *pray* what we read, working our lives into active participation in what God reveals in the word. God does not expect us to take this new reality lying down. We'd better *not* take it lying down, for God intends that this word get us on our feet walking, running, singing.

God doesn't make us do any of this: God's word is personal address, inviting, commanding, challenging, rebuking, judging, comforting, directing. But not forcing. Not coercing. We are given space and freedom to answer, to enter into the conversation. From beginning to end, the word of God is a dialogical word, a word that invites participation. Prayer is our participation in the creation, salvation, and community that God reveals to us in Holy Scripture.

Contemplatio

The final and completing element in *lectio divina* is contemplation. Contemplation in the schema of *lectio divina* means living the read/meditated/prayed text in the everyday, ordinary world. It means getting the text into our muscles and bones, our oxygen-breathing lungs and blood-pumping heart. But if we are going to use the word in this com-

18. Julian Green, *Diaries* (New York: Macmillan, 1955), p. 101.

prehensive and everyday way, we need first to free it from its stereo-typed meaning. The common American stereotype of contemplation is that it is what monks and nuns do in monasteries and convents. Serious contemplation involves leaving the world of family and domesticity, of city and business, taking vows of poverty, chastity, and obedience in order to live in quiet prayerfulness and reflective study, undistracted in the presence of God. Historically, the word is rightly used in referring to such lives, but not *only* to such lives. Even though for fifteen hundred years and more, many, maybe most, of the men and women who used the word "contemplation" lived in such settings, there is nothing in the practice itself that requires a vowed life of seclusion from the "world." Still, it is hard to free our imaginations from the extensive associations derived from the writings of the desert fathers and mothers in Egypt, Teresa of Avila in her Carmelite convent in Spain, Benedict and his monks in the monastery at Monte Cassino, Hildegard leading her nuns in the convent she founded at Bingen (Germany), Bernard preaching to his monks at Clairvaux, or, in our day, Thomas Merton with the Trappists in Kentucky. In these contexts the contemplative life is almost always set in contrast to the active life, which is understood as life outside the monastery and convent. Hans Urs von Balthasar, the Roman Catholic theologian who gave a lifetime to the study and practice of the contemplative life, does his best to counter the falsifying stereotype by naming contemplation as a "link" which ties worship in the sanctuary and work in the world in a bundle that is at once secular and sacred: "The life of contemplation is perforce an everyday life, of small fidelities and services performed in the spirit of love, which lightens our tasks and gives to them its warmth."[19]

I have no argument with or criticism of the contemplation that is practiced in the monasteries; in fact, I am endlessly grateful for the men and women who gave (and continue to give!) themselves to such disciplined attentiveness to our Lord. But I am also determined to do what I can to get the term "contemplation" into circulation in the

19. Hans Urs von Balthasar, *Prayer*, trans. A. V. Littledale (London: Geoffrey Chapman, 1963), p. 111.

world of the everyday, what Kathleen Norris calls "The quotidian mysteries: laundry, liturgy and 'women's work.'" She writes,

> I have come to believe that the true mystics of the quotidian are not those who contemplate holiness in isolation, reaching godlike illumination in serene silence, but those who manage to find God in a life filled with noise, the demands of other people and relentless daily duties that can consume the self. They may be young parents juggling child-rearing and making a living. . . . [I]f they are wise, they treasure the rare moments of solitude and silence that come their way, and use them not to escape, to distract themselves with television and the like. Instead, they listen for a sign of God's presence and they open their hearts toward prayer.[20]

I stake my claim for the democratization of contemplation on the observation that virtually all children up to the age of three to five years are natural contemplatives: unself-consciously present to the immediate flower, absorbed and oblivious while watching an ant track its way across a log.

Denise Levertov, writing as a poet, understands contemplation as native ground for all who take words seriously by calling attention to the Oxford English Dictionary's definition of contemplation as coming from "*templum,* temple, a place for observation, marked out by the augur." It means, she says, "not simply to observe, to regard, but to do these things *in the presence of a god.*"[21] It means becoming aware of the total surrounding context — reflecting on human presence in a divine atmosphere. The lexical territory in which Levertov stakes her claim is poetry — she is a poet working with words. As a reader working with the words of Scripture, I am likewise determined to recover the words of Scripture as a *templum,* and then live these words that I read "in the

---

20. Kathleen Norris, *The Quotidian Mysteries* (New York: Paulist, 1998), pp. 1, 70.

21. Denise Levertov, *The Poet in the World* (New York: New Directions, 1973), p. 8, my emphasis.

presence of a god," in my case the God and Father of our Lord Jesus Christ.[22]

If *lectio divina* is to have currency in the Christian community today, contemplation simply must be reclaimed as essential in all reading and living of Scripture. It is not an option; it is necessary. The word's very strangeness and remoteness from the ordinary may even be an advantage in recovering its distinctive punch: it administers a verbal jolt to our ears, surprising us out of our hurried, harried, self-defeating addictions to what we have become used to calling fulfillment and the pursuit of happiness — our American culture's emasculated version of heaven. As such it functions nicely as a protest word against so much of what is held up for admiration and emulation among us: spiritual technology, psychological manipulation, institutionalized control, sanctioned addictions, evangelical hurry, messianic violence, pious indulgence.

Contemplation means submitting to the biblical revelation, taking it within ourselves, and then living it unpretentiously, without fanfare. It doesn't mean (and these are the stereotyped misunderstandings) quiet, withdrawn, secluded, serene, or benign. It has nothing to do with whether we spend our days as a grease monkey under an automobile or on our knees in a Benedictine choir. It doesn't mean "having it all together." It doesn't mean being emotionally and mentally well-balanced.

Contemplatives fly off the handle, make bad judgments, speak out mistakenly and regret their words, run stoplights and get speeding tickets. Contemplatives get depressed, get confused, get fat, get lost, and sometimes don't get it at all. "Contemplative" is not a term of achievement. It is not a badge of merit.

Contemplative is a designation that any one of us can accept for ourselves and one that we all should. We will never read and live the Bi-

---

22. I am not alone in this. There is a growing company of others who are likewise determined to make the word and all that it means available to every Christian, regardless of his or her place in the world. For me, the clearest and most comprehensive witness comes from Hans Urs von Balthasar in his *Prayer*.

ble rightly if we don't. *Lectio divina* anticipates and assumes contemplation. If it makes us feel better to attach the adjective "failed" I have no objection. Failed contemplative. All contemplatives are failed contemplatives. But the word itself, whether as adjective or noun, stands: contemplative.

Contemplation means living what we read, not wasting any of it or hoarding any of it, but using it up in living. It is life formed by God's revealing word, God's word read and heard, meditated and prayed. The contemplative life is not a special kind of life; it is the Christian life, nothing more but also nothing less. But *lived*. Joseph Conrad captured the essence of the contemplative life when he called attention to

> that part of our being which is a gift, not an acquisition, to the capacity for delight and wonder . . . our sense of pity and pain, to the latent feeling of fellowship with all creation — and to the subtle but invincible conviction of solidarity that knits together the loneliness of innumerable hearts . . . which binds together all humanity — the dead to the living and the living to the unborn.[23]

Contemplative is not an elitist category of Christian. The importance of rehabilitating the word is that our culture has taken to using "Christian" to refer to virtually anybody who is not a communist or a criminal. We need an unpopular word that kicks off some awareness of what is odd in those who live by faith in Jesus Christ, a verbal tool that calls attention to what is distinctive in this word-of-God-formed life. Maybe the awkwardness of this word in the climate of this age will signpost resistance to the acids of secularism that erode the sharp edges of our identity in Christ.

Contemplative in the context of *lectio divina*, our spiritual reading of the Holy Scriptures, signals a recognition of an organic union between the word "read" and the word "lived." The contemplative life is

---

23. Quoted by Saul Bellow in his 1976 Nobel Lecture in *It All Adds Up* (New York: Penguin, 1995), pp. 88-89.

the realization that the Word that was in the beginning is also the Word made flesh and continues to be the Word to which I say, *Fiat mihi:* "Let it be to *me* according to thy Word."

The assumption underlying contemplation is that Word and Life are at root the same thing. Life originates in Word. Word makes Life. There is no word of God that God does not intend to be lived by us. All words are capable of being incarnated, because all words originate in the Word made flesh.

All words are likewise capable of dis-carnation, of not conceiving life in our flesh and blood, of being turned into lies. The Devil, according to some of our best teachers, is discarnate — incapable of getting into flesh, into life. The Devil's only way of getting into the world's affairs is by using us as "carriers." The Devil needs human flesh to do his work. Because the Devil is completely otherworldly, so un*Wordly*, he has no capacity for "on earth as it is in Hell" except as we flesh and blood people speak his lies and act out his illusions.

The refusal, whether intentional or inadvertent, to embrace the contemplative life leaves us exposed to becoming carriers of the Devil's lies, disincarnating God's words in the very act of blithely and piously quoting Holy Scripture. For every word of God revealed and read in the Bible is there to be conceived and born in us: Christ, the Word made flesh, made flesh in our flesh.

A word is not something spiritual as opposed to something material. Everything about a word is material: it begins as a puff of air, is put in motion by the contraction of our lungs, is pushed up the tunnel of the esophagus through the constrictions of larynx and pharynx, and is then worked on by that excellent trio, tongue, teeth, and lips, to make a word. That is not the end of the physicalness, the materiality, of word. Air composed of a combination of named gases, mixed with a variety of pollutants in the air we breathe, transmits the word to our ears along paths, these incredible miniature ear miracles of engineering, paths that are just as physical as any concrete bridge or asphalt roadway. The word bangs against a membrane and activates tiny acoustical gears that drive the sound into the synapses of the brain, at which point we repent of our sins or believe in Jesus or love our enemy or visit the sick, any one of which actions is physical: word into flesh. Meister Eckhart (d. 1327), the Dominican preacher in Germany, famously put contemplation in this earthy context in a sermon: "if a man were in rapture like Saint Paul, and knew a sick man who needed some soup from him, I should think it far better if you abandoned rapture for love."[24]

"Word into flesh" doesn't mean the spiritual into the physical. The word is already physical; it means into *Jesus'* flesh. Particular, local, named flesh. And when we pray, "Let it be done to me according to thy word," we mean for it to take place in our flesh; a miraculous conception in the womb of our lives, "Christ in me," the word as materially present as the paths that we walk, the word both as obvious and as mysterious as the light that shines from the lamps we hold.

Denis Donoghue, one of our best literary critics, once commented that when William Carlos Williams, one of our very best poets, "saw a footprint he had no interest in the meaning of the experience as knowledge, perception, vision, or even truth: he just wanted to find the foot."[25] This is what contemplatives do, look around and within for the foot that fits the (Scripture) footprint.

Contemplatio, unlike its three companions, is not something we self-consciously do; it happens, it is a gift, it is something to which we are receptive and obedient. In the language of our tradition, it is "infused." Contemplation "is not something we can produce or practice. . . . We can be ready for it, we can prepare for it, we cannot, however, elicit it. . . ."[26] We do not become contemplative before Scripture by turning toward it as object, by an active intellect at work on the object, organizing and analyzing. It can only be "the knowledge of love, of desire and delight, the will consenting to the drawing of the divine beauty."[27]

24. Quoted by Rowan Williams, *Christian Spirituality* (Atlanta: John Knox, 1980), p. 134.

25. Denis Donoghue, *The Ordinary Universe* (New York: Macmillan, 1968), p. 182.

26. Andrew Louth, *The Origins of the Christian Mystical Tradition* (Oxford: Clarendon, 1981), p. 14.

27. Rowan Williams discussing Augustine: *Christian Spirituality,* p. 74.

Contemplation is not another thing added on to our reading and meditating and praying but the coming together of God's revelation and our response, an unself-conscious following of Jesus, a Jesus-coherent life. It is not thinking about God, not asking continuously "what would Jesus do?" but jumping into the river; not strategizing the success of my life but just being myself, my Christ-in-me-life; not calculating effects but accepting and submitting to on-earth-as-it-is-in-heaven conditions.

And that means that most contemplation is unnoticed, unremarked, unself-conscious. So much of the word of God is revealed in silence, hiddenness, and mystery[28] that chances are, even if we have been rubbing shoulders with a contemplative all our life, we wouldn't know it. It is even more unlikely that we will ever recognize a contemplative in a mirror.

The impossibility of evaluation, at least self-evaluation, releases us into a great freedom as we read these Holy Scriptures and struggle and enjoy and receive them. We will not try too hard. We will not set ourselves perfectionist goals. We won't take over. We won't insist on measured progress. We won't compete. Having read and meditated and prayed, and continuing to read and meditate and pray, we will step back and bless, love and obey, and breathe "let it be to me according to your word." Relax and receive.

Once more: *caveat lector.*

Lectio divina is not a methodical technique for reading the Bible. It is a cultivated, developed habit of *living* the text in Jesus' name. This is the way, the *only* way, that the Holy Scriptures become formative in the Christian church and become salt and leaven in the world. It is not through doctrinal disputes and formulations, not through strategies to subdue the barbarians, not through congregational programs to educate the laity in the "principles and truths" of the Scriptures — not in any of the ways in which the Bible is so commonly and vigorously pro-

28. For an accurate, passionate exposition of this see Virginia Stem Owens, *The Total Image* (Grand Rapids: Eerdmans, 1980), especially pp. 39-61.

moted among us as an impersonal weapon or tool or program. It is astonishing how many ways we manage to devise for using the Bible to avoid a believing obedience, both personal and corporate, in receiving and following the Word made flesh.

Yes, by all means: *Beware.*

III

THE COMPANY
OF TRANSLATORS

*"How is it that we hear, each of us, in our own native language . . .
hear them speaking about God's deeds of power?"*

ACTS 2:8, 11 NRSV

*"Every translation is a messianic act, which brings redemption
nearer."*

FRANZ ROSENZWEIG

CHAPTER 8

God's Secretaries

The overwhelming majority of men and women who have heard and/
or read the word of God as revealed in Scripture and by proclamation
have done it with the help of a vast company of translators. Apart from
the translators, most of them anonymous, there would be precious little reading and hearing of the word of God. Our Bible is the most
translated book in the world.

The identity of Jesus — "King of the Jews" — as he hung on the
cross on Golgotha was placarded by Pilate in the three languages in
common use that day in Jerusalem: Aramaic,[1] Latin, and Greek. There
is considerable irony in the fact that Pontius Pilate, the Roman gover-
nor who condemned Jesus to that crucifixion death, ordered and had
translated the words that announced, even if not quite in the way he intended, Jesus' sovereignty (John 19:19-20). We don't often think of Pilate in the company of translators, but there it is.

Translation of Scripture became necessary several hundred years
before the time of Jesus and the early church when its original language, Hebrew, was gradually replaced in the everyday lives of the people of God first by Aramaic and then by Greek.

---

1. When the New Testament Greek text (and many translations) reads "Hebrew"
here it almost certainly intends "Aramaic," a sister language to Hebrew.

Translation into Aramaic

Translation into Aramaic played a decisive role in the years following Israel's return from Babylonian exile in the sixth century B.C. In 538 B.C. the liberal-minded Persian leader, Cyrus, released Israel from their years of exile, freeing them to return to their homeland in Palestine. Aramaic was the official language of the Persian empire. Over the years, the many local languages represented in that gargantuan expanse of real estate ("from India to Ethiopia," in the comprehensive phrase that opens the book of Esther), languages that included Israel's Hebrew, were pushed to the sidelines by Aramaic, the official language of government and business.

By the time Pilate added his two cents' worth of translation to Jesus' cross, Hebrew had probably ceased to be the spoken language of daily life in most areas, replaced by Aramaic, the same Aramaic that served as the primary language of Jesus and his early followers. Aramaic as the dominant language of Jesus and his first followers is obscured for us because it is so meagerly represented in our Bibles.

In the Old Testament Aramaic accounts for a few pages of Ezra (4:8–6:18 and 7:12-26), a little over half of Daniel (2:4–7:22), two words in Genesis (31:47), one word in the Psalms (2:12), and one verse in Jeremiah (10:11).

In the New Testament a bare twenty-one words or phrases are the only traces remaining from the richly layered deposits of the language that Jesus and his early disciples spoke: ten words or phrases from the Gospel writers and Paul: *raca* (Matt. 5:22), *satanas* (Matt. 16:23), *talitha koum* (Mark 5:41), *ephphatha* (Mark 7:34), *pascha* (Mark 14:1), *abba* (Mark 14:36; Rom. 8:15), *eloi, eloi, lama sabachthani* (Mark 15:34), *Messias* (John 1:41), *rabboni* (John 20:16), *marana tha* (1 Cor. 16:22);[2] three Aramaic place names, Golgotha, Gabbatha, and Akeldama (John 19:13, 17; Acts 1:19); and eight Aramaic personal names, Cephas,

2. *Mammon* ("that in which one puts his trust," from the same root as "Amen"), a word Jesus used to refer to money, is possibly Aramaic. If it is included the count the would be twenty-two.

Bartholomew, Bartimaeus, Barnabas, Martha, Thomas, Thaddeus, and Barabbas. That's it.

Among the Dead Sea Scrolls, some of which can be dated to the mid third century B.C., sixty-one items translated into Aramaic, including a fragment of the biblical book of Job, would seem to confirm the "widespread and predominant use of Aramaic" during the intertestamental years.[3]

We get a glimpse of the beginning of this process of transition from Hebrew to Aramaic in the story of Ezra and Nehemiah. The time was roughly 450 B.C.[4] Ezra and Nehemiah had come from the eastern parts of the Persian empire to Jerusalem to rally the demoralized Jews who had returned from their Babylonian exile. But what had been anticipated as a glorious return to their homeland and a triumphant rebuilding of the destroyed Solomonic temple had fizzled. On arrival their imaginations were electric with Isaiah's visionary preaching of the exile:

> It is too light a thing that you should be my servant
>> to raise up the tribes of Jacob
>> and to restore the survivors of Israel;
> I will give you as a light to the nations,
>> that my salvation may reach to the end of the earth.
>
> (Isa. 49:6 NRSV)

That vaulting hope with which they had arrived back in Palestine, expecting to be "a light to the nations," soon dissipated. Many of their brothers and sisters in exile, comfortably established in Babylon, had

3. Emil Schurer, *The History of the Jewish People in the Age of Jesus Christ*, revised by Geza Vermes, Fergus Millar, and Matthew Black (Edinburgh: T & T Clark, 1979), vol. 2, pp. 22-23.

4. The chronology of Ezra-Nehemiah is much discussed and argued by scholars. We can place them roughly in the quarter century of 450 to 425 B.C. — in round numbers, a hundred years after the first returnees from Babylonian exile. See I. W. Provan, V. P. Long, and T. Longman III, *A Biblical History of Israel* (Louisville: Westminster/John Knox, 2003), pp. 285-303.

refused to return with them. The returnees experienced years of drought and bad crops, had meager resources, and were cruelly harassed by their Samaritan neighbors to the north. It looked very much as if the community would not make it. Year after year after year of unrelieved struggle had unraveled the grand tapestry of Isaianic visions; their identity as God's people was hanging by the merest thread.

Rescuing help came with the arrival first of Ezra and then of Nehemiah, both of whom held prominent positions in the Persian government. When they learned of the desperate straits of their Palestinian brothers and sisters they set out to rally their spirits. It is no exaggeration to say that these two men were as crucial to the survival of the people of God as Moses was to their formation. They did precisely what was necessary to re-establish the community's identity as a people of God and set them on the way in which they have continued ever since. Ezra reformed their spiritual life; Nehemiah pulled them together politically, rebuilding their defenses.

Ezra arrived with a copy of the Law of Moses written in its original Hebrew. Through the decades of poverty and harassment, these troubled Jews eking out a bare existence in Jerusalem had lost touch with their past — lost the memory of the Moses-led salvation, lost intimacy with the Sinai revelation, lost connection with the wilderness disciplines, lost touch with the family stories of Abraham and Sarah, Ruth and Boaz, David and Abigail. Ezra knew that he needed to start back at square one. He would start with the Scriptures. He had a wooden platform constructed in the town square, gathered the people together, mounted the platform, and began reading from the Hebrew scroll, reading them the story of who they were and where they had come from, their identity and their destiny.

But there was a problem. The people who had lost touch with their past had also lost touch with their language. Hebrew, while most of them most certainly understood it, was no longer their first language, their cradle tongue. In the hundred and thirty or so years since their ancestors had been exiled to Babylon (586 B.C.) their Hebrew had receded to the margins of their lives. They had grown up speaking Aramaic, the *lingua franca* of the Persian empire, as had their parents and grandparents going back several generations. And Aramaic would continue to be their primary language long into the future, into the time of Jesus.

It became apparent that Ezra's grand identity-recovering enterprise that day required interpretive help. Luckily, the Levites, the priestly class responsible for staying in touch with their ancient Moses roots, were still completely at home in Hebrew. So as Ezra read from the scroll written in Hebrew, thirteen Levites placed strategically throughout the assembled congregation "gave the sense, so that the people understood the reading" (Neh. 8:8). "Gave the sense" was probably not translation in a strict sense, but more like assisting the people by explaining and interpreting what Ezra was reading from this long neglected and now unfamiliar text. What seems to have been going on that day is that this post-exilic community in Jerusalem needed *interpretive* help in listening to the Hebrew Bible that would also involve the occasional translation of a Hebrew word or phrase into the Aramaic that by this time was in process of replacing Hebrew as the vernacular language in Palestine.

But "gave the sense" did more than merely provide dictionary equivalents to the words that were being read that day. The Levites' interpretive translation work engaged the *lives*, the hearts and souls, not just the minds, of the people: at first they wept and then they rejoiced "because they had understood the words that were declared to them" (Neh. 8:9-12). This is the intended end of true translation, to bring about the kind of understanding that involves the whole person in tears and laughter, heart and soul, in what is written, what is said.[5]

These thirteen men are not otherwise mentioned in the biblical story but neither are they quite anonymous. As Ezra's assistants, they saved the day by using the everyday vernacular to interpret and clarify Ezra's reading of God's word for a people of God who at that moment

---

5. Much attention has been given in our day to this complex and comprehensive work of interpretation. "Hermeneutics" labels the discipline. For a thoroughgoing account see Anthony Thiselton, *The Two Horizons* (Grand Rapids: Eerdmans, 1980), and Paul Ricoeur, *Essays in Biblical Interpretation* (Philadelphia: Fortress, 1980).

hardly knew what "people of God" meant, let alone that it meant *them*. These men at least deserve the dignity of being named among us again. Here they are: Jeshua, Bani, Sherebiah, Jamin, Akkub, Shabbethai, Hodiah, Maaseiah, Kelita, Azariah, Jozabad, Hanan, Pelaiah (Neh. 8:7). The thirteen interpreters orally supplied the necessary connection — Aramaic! — between past and present that day. Because they "gave the sense" so the people could understand the meaning, the people of God would continue for the next four hundred years or so to use Aramaic, into the time when Jesus would hang on a cross in Jerusalem, identified as their King in this same Aramaic language.[6]

Translation into Greek

The translation of the Hebrew Bible into Greek is our first complete translation. Whereas in translation into Aramaic we have only bits and pieces, fragments scattered here and there and, as in the story of Ezra and the thirteen Levites, something only anticipatory and suggestive, the translation of the Scriptures into Greek is complete, the entire Hebrew Bible — and then some — well before the time of Jesus and the descent of the Holy Spirit at Pentecost.

As it turned out, this Greek translation was *the* Bible of the first Christian church, their "authorized" version. When Paul wrote his letters to the newly formed Christian communities and quoted from the Bible to authenticate and confirm the common relationship of these early Christians with the people of God who had been redeemed from Egyptian slavery, trained into a life of love and obedience in wilderness and promised land, and instructed and challenged by the great preaching prophets of Israel, he almost always quoted from this Greek translation. When Mark wrote his groundbreaking Gospel, he made 68 dis-

6. Translation into Aramaic for centuries was mostly oral. But eventually there were written translations. The culmination of this process took place in Babylon in the fifth century A.D. with official rabbinic Targumim ("translations") in Aramaic. See F. F. Bruce, *The Books and the Parchments*, revised ed. (London: Marshall Pickering, 1991), pp. 123-35.

tinct references to the Old Testament of which 25 are exact or nearly exact quotations from the Greek translation. When Paul and Silas arrived in the Greek town of Beroea and had a Bible study with some Jews in the synagogue there, "examining the scriptures daily to see if these things [the gospel] were so," it was undoubtedly the official Greek translation of the "scriptures" that they studied (Acts 17:10-12). Many centuries later when Walter Bauer wrote his introduction to what has become the standard lexicon of New Testament Greek, he said, "As for the influence of the LXX [the Greek translation], every page of this lexicon shows that it outweighs all other influences on our literature."[7]

Just as translation into Aramaic had become necessary in the years following Cyrus's decree that Aramaic would be the official language of the huge and multi-languaged Persian empire, so two hundred years later translation into Greek became necessary when Alexander the Great conquered everything Persian and nearly overnight (as history goes) turned everyone into Greeks, or at least people who spoke Greek. As Aramaic had become the *lingua franca* of Cyrus's Persian empire, so Greek became the *lingua franca* of Alexander's Greek empire. And for the same reason — in order to run a government and conduct business with such a diverse population speaking so many tongues (a regular Babel it was), there had to be a common language. This time the Greeks were in charge, so the language was Greek.

But something else had happened in that two hundred years. In the time between Cyrus and Alexander, the Jewish community had gradually been dispersed all over the Persian/Greek world. The dispersion that had begun under the Babylonians was reversed by the Persians, whose policy was to repatriate exiled peoples to their homelands so they could rebuild their places of worship.[8] This back-and-

---

7. *A Greek-English Lexicon of the New Testament and Other Early Christian Literature*, third English ed., revised and edited by Frederick William Danker (Chicago: University of Chicago Press, 2000), p. xxii.

8. Strikingly documented in the Cyrus Cylinder, a cuneiform inscription. Translation in *Ancient Near Eastern Texts*, ed. James Pritchard (Princeton, N.J.: Princeton University Press, 1955), p. 316.

forthness weakened any sense of place, further stirring the huge dispersion melting-pot. The process of dispersion was continued by the Greeks, who were great colonizers. Under their rule the Jews, earlier uprooted and later restored to Palestine, learned to make themselves at home virtually anywhere. After a hundred years or so of Greek rule, there were Jews in most of the major cities of the Mediterranean and Middle Eastern world. Wherever they landed they established a synagogue, faithfully nurturing in the soil of their Holy Scriptures (the only soil left to them) their identity as God's people. Two years into his blitzkrieg that would take him all the way from Macedonia to India in ten years, Alexander the Great conquered Egypt and immediately created a new city there in his own honor. The year was 332 B.C. In typical Alexandrian hubris he named it Alexandria. Within a couple of generations Greek-speaking Jews made up one third of the city's inhabitants and outnumbered the Jews in Jerusalem. The Jewish population continued to multiply not only in Alexandria but throughout the Greek empire. Every decade removed the Jews further from the language of their Scriptures. They needed their Bible in Greek for reading in the synagogues.

So it is fitting that the initiative for translating the Bible into Greek took place in Alexandria. The story is told in *The Letter of Aristeas*, a kernel of historic fact elaborated into a legend. But the legend is worth telling for what it conveys to us of the Jewish regard for translation as such. Aristeas, the legend goes, held high office in the court of Ptolemy II (285-247 B.C.), who was a great patron of learning with a library of more than two hundred thousand books. The story Aristeas tells is that Demetrius, the royal librarian of Ptolemy, informed the king that the Jews had valuable books that deserved a place in the library. The king gave him the go-ahead. Demetrius told him that these books were in an odd script and would require translation. So the king ordered that a letter be sent to Eleazar, high priest in Jerusalem, to acquire the manuscripts accompanied by translators. The high priest selected six elders from each of the twelve tribes as translators. When the seventy-two elders arrived in Alexandria, the king treated them to a sumptuous banquet and tested them with hard questions. They passed muster and three days later were taken by the librarian Demetrius to the island of Pharos (famous for its lighthouse), offshore from Alexandria, and put to work in a building that had been prepared for them. They went to work and in seventy-two days the seventy-two elders had completed the work. Seventy-two was rounded off to seventy and the translation has been called the *Septuagint* (seventy, in Roman numerals LXX) ever since.

The legend, as legends do, developed. Later tellers of the tale recounted that the seventy-two each worked independently in a separate cell without seeing or talking to one another. At the end of the seventy-two days all the versions were found to be word-for-word identical.

The legend entertains, as legends are supposed to do. But the kernel of fact is indisputable: the translation of the Bible into Greek that was made in Alexandria during the reign of Ptolemy II became the official Bible of the far-flung Jewish communities and eventually of the beginning Christian church.[9]

But the significance of the *Letter* for us is the enormous respect and honor in the Jewish (and later Christian) community that was given to this translation and its translators. They believed that the same Spirit of God at work in the writing of Scripture is also at work in the translating of Scripture. A hundred years or so after the *Letter*, Philo, an Alexandrian Jew contemporary with Jesus, without referring to the *Letter*, gave a similar evaluation of the translation, designating the original writing of Scripture in Hebrew and the translation of Scripture into Greek as "sisters." Jews, he wrote, who are bilingual in Hebrew and Greek

> regard them [the original and the translation] with awe and reverence as sisters, or rather as one and the same, both in matter and words, and speak of the authors not as translators but as prophets

9. The *Letter of Aristeas* refers only to translating the Torah, the first five books of Moses. The rest of the Old Testament was done piecemeal over the next hundred years or so. By the beginning of the Christian era the whole Hebrew Bible was complete in Greek translation.

and priests of the mysteries . . . hand in hand with the purest of spirits, the spirit of Moses.[10]

For both Jews and Christians the original and the translation were on a par with one another as authoritative Scripture.

Translation into American

Two thousand years later I found myself in the company of translators, but without any self-awareness that I was a translator. I was a pastor in America. My work involved calling the two to three hundred people who made up my congregation to worship and serving them the Eucharist. I preached sermons and taught Bible studies, I prayed with and for them, I visited the sick and cared for souls, I baptized and confirmed, I married and buried. We were all fluent in American English. Who needed a translator with these people and under these circumstances?

And yet I often found myself identifying with Ezra's thirteen Levites in post-exilic Jerusalem. George Steiner in his wide-ranging treatment of translation, *After Babel*, convinces that translation *within* a language (intralingual) is on a continuum with translation *between* languages (interlingual).[11] I was most conscious of being in the company of the Levites when I was in the pulpit, attempting to make the Scriptures understandable in the colloquial language of the day. Just as the Levites assisted Ezra in Judah by "giving the sense" for understanding the Bible in those post-exilic days of a rapidly disintegrating biblical culture, I was doing something very similar as a pastor in postmodern American, for neither was my congregation familiar with their past, with their Scriptures, their biblically formed identity. In parallel with the Levites using vernacular Aramaic, most of my "transla-

---

10. Quoted in C. K. Barrett, ed., *The New Testament Background: Selected Documents*, revised ed. (London: SPCK, 1987), p. 294.

11. George Steiner, *After Babel* (New York: Oxford University Press, 1975).

tion" was also oral, giving the interpretation, the "understanding," of the Scriptures as they were read out in the sanctuary to my assembled congregation, and also providing an occasional American equivalent to an unfamiliar idiom or metaphor.

And then something happened that without my being aware of its significance at the time put me in the company of translators. It took place in the early 1980s in our small town twenty miles from the city of Baltimore. A financial downturn had raised anxieties among many in my mostly middle-class congregation. Race riots flaring up in many of the cities of America including nearby Baltimore exacerbated the anxiety. The entire community in which I lived and worked was suddenly security conscious. Neighbors were double-locking their doors and installing alarm systems. Men and women who had never held a gun were buying guns. Racial fears developed into racial slurs. Paranoia infected the small talk I would overhear on street corners and in barbershops. To my dismay, all of this seeped into my congregation without encountering any resistance.

My dismay soon turned to anger. How could this congregation of Christians so unthinkingly absorb the world's fearful anxiety and hateful distrust — and so easily? Overnight, it seemed, they had turned their homes into armed camps. They were living defensively, guardedly, timidly. And they were Christians! I had been their pastor for twenty years, preaching the good news that Jesus had overcome the world, defining their neighbor with Jesus' story of the good Samaritan, defending them against the status quo with Jesus' story of the cautious servant who buried his talent. I had led them in Bible studies that I had supposed were grounding them in the freedom for which Christ had set us free, keeping their feet firmly in, "but not of," the world around us for which Christ died. And here they were, before my eyes, paralyzed by fear and "anxious for the morrow."

As my anger and dismay subsided, I began plotting a pastoral strategy that I hoped would recover their identity as a free people in Christ, a people not "conformed to the world" but living robustly and spontaneously in the Spirit. Galatians seemed a good place to start. I was angry and this was Paul's angriest letter, provoked by a report that

Christian congregations that Paul had formed a few years before had abandoned the life of freedom for the security system of the old Jewish codes. I thought it was Galatians-time for my congregation. The secure and cautious conditions of suburbia had softened and blurred the sharp edges of the gospel and left them undefended against the anxieties of the day. I thought that the parallel between our congregations, Paul's in Galatia and mine in Maryland, was exquisitely serendipitous, and I was going to make the most it.

But I also knew that this was going to take awhile. I decided that I would teach an adult class on Galatians for a year and follow that up by a year of preaching through Galatians. I was going to soak them in Galatians. They were going to have Galatians coming out their pores. After two years they wouldn't know whether they were living in Galatia or America. But they were going to know something about freedom, the freedom for which Christ set them free.

I announced an adult class for the study of Galatians to the congregation. Our adult church-school class met in the basement of our educational wing on Sunday mornings, bare cement block walls, folding chairs, a horseshoe arrangement of vinyl-surfaced tables, an easel of newsprint — our suburban Presbyterian equivalent of the catacombs. I had always loved the intimacy and leisure of these gatherings, the immersion in Scripture, the experiences of surprise and recognition — God's word! — and the ambience of honesty and revelation that always seemed to develop. As we set ourselves in the arena of God's revelation, moments always seemed to occur when first one, then another, would become capable of revealing herself, himself, cautiously edging out from behind the disguises and make-up by which we all attempt to make ourselves respectable and acceptable in the world.

On the Sunday set for the beginning of the study, fourteen men and women showed up, my usual take from our congregation. My routine was to arrive early, brew an urn of coffee, prepare hot water for tea, put out the condiments and Styrofoam cups, spread Bibles out on the tables. Small talk consumed the first few minutes as we got our coffee and took our places around the tables. I always felt that for the first ten minutes or so the Bibles on the table were competing for attention with the liturgical act of stirring cream and sugar into the coffee cups; most Sundays the Bible would eventually pull out in front, but on this particular Sunday those white Styrofoam cups seemed to be winning. Here I was laying the groundwork for a major renewal of Spirit-torched imagination in my congregation. Galatians, Paul's angry, passionate, fiery letter that rescued his congregation from their regression to culture slavery, was on the table and nobody was getting it. Sweetly smiling, they were giving more attention to stirring sugar into those Styrofoam cups than to the Spirit words that pulsed in Paul's metaphors and syntax. It was obvious that they weren't getting it. And I was offended, mightily offended.

I don't know why I was particularly struck that day, for it happens all the time: parents with children, friends with friends, pastors with parishioners, teachers with students, coaches with players. We get hold of something that turns life inside out — a truth-probing idea, a blaze of beauty, a passionate love — and urgently press our discovery on another person. After a short time of polite listening, the person, obviously bored, either wanders away or changes the subject, not unlike those times as an adolescent when we fell totally in love with another and couldn't wait to tell our best friend. Whereupon our friend said, "I don't know what you see in him, in her." Here we have just discovered this extravagantly beautiful person, every sentence coming from his lips a melody, every step she takes a figure in a dance, and our friend, our *best* friend, says, "I don't know what you see in her."

That is how I felt that Sunday morning in that Presbyterian basement room in Maryland. They were reading sentences that charted a revolution — and stirring sugar into their coffee.

Later in the afternoon, I told my wife of the sputtery morning launch of the Galatians study. Frustrated and fuming I said, "I know what I'm going to do; I'm going to teach them Greek — if they read it in Greek, those sweet smiles will vanish soon enough. If they read it in Greek, Paul's somersaulting, cartwheeling, freedom-trumpeting Greek, they'll get it." She gave me one of her sweet smiles and said, "I can't think of a better way to empty out the classroom."

The smile did it. I abandoned the Greek project. What I did instead was spend the week doodling with Paul's Greek, trying to turn it into how I thought it sounded in American English. I tried to imagine Paul as pastor to these people who were letting their hard-won freedom in Christ slip through their fingers. How would he write to them in the language they used when they weren't in church? I had no plan, no program, nothing ambitious like Greek. I just wanted them to hear it the way I heard it, the way the Galatians heard it, the way Luther heard it, the way so many men and women through our Christian centuries have heard it and found themselves set free by and for God.

The next Sunday I brewed the coffee and heated the water for tea as I always did, but I omitted the Bibles. Instead of Bibles I had fourteen copies of my doodles — one page double-spaced, about 250 words — spread out on the tables. And I read:

I, Paul, and my companions in faith here, send greetings to the Galatian churches. My authority for writing to you does not come from any popular vote of the people, nor does it come through the appointment of some human higher-up. It comes directly from Jesus the Messiah and God the Father, who raised him from the dead. I'm God-commissioned. So I greet you with the great words, grace and peace! We know the meaning of those words because Jesus Christ rescued us from this evil world we're in by offering himself as a sacrifice for our sins. God's plan is that we all experience that rescue. Glory to God forever! Oh, yes!

I can't believe your fickleness — how easily you have turned traitor to him who called you by the grace of Christ by embracing a variant message! It is not a minor variation, you know; it is completely other, an alien message, a no-message, a lie about God. Those who are provoking this agitation among you are turning the Message of Christ on its head. Let me be blunt: If one of us — even an angel from heaven! — were to preach something other than what we preached originally, let him be cursed. I said it once; I'll say it again: If anyone, regardless of reputation or credentials, preaches something other than what you received originally, let him be cursed.

And so it continued. We went over the pages week after week, trying to get Paul's Greek into the American that they spoke when they weren't in church, the words and phrases they used when they were at work on the job, at home playing with their children, out on the street. Every week I brought in another page. We tested the metaphors and phrasings against American English, suggested emendations, threw out clichés, all the time trying to preserve the sharp edge of Paul's language in our vernacular.

After the second week of using this new format, as I was cleaning and straightening up the room, I noticed that all the Styrofoam coffee cups were half-full of cold coffee. I knew I had them. I've never taken so much satisfaction in cleaning up after guests — pouring all that cold coffee into the sink and pitching their cups into the waste can!

We pored over a freshly xeroxed copy of the translated text every Sunday morning through that autumn, winter, and spring. In nine months we had completed Galatians. Without knowing what we were doing, or the impact it would make on our culture, we had joined the company of translators, "God's secretaries."[12] The next autumn I set out on a nine-month course of preaching this same Galatians text to the worshipping congregation. The following summer I started writing, hoping to make a book of these two years of Galatians conversations and prayer, worship and teaching, pastor-and-congregation collaboration in listening to the Spirit's great freedom text, recovering and submitting ourselves and our culture to God's shaping word.

Several years after the book was published,[13] I received a letter from an editor. "Do you remember that book you wrote on Galatians? Well, I photocopied the translation portions, taped them together, and have been carrying them around ever since, reading them over and

12. The title of Adam Nicolson's book on the work of the company of translators, the fifty or so scholars and pastors, who translated the King James Bible in the seven years 1604 to 1611 (New York: HarperCollins, 2003).

13. *Traveling Light: Modern Meditations on St. Paul's Letter of Freedom* (Colorado Springs: Helmers and Howard, 1988; first published as *Traveling Light: Reflections on the Free Life*, by InterVarsity Press, 1982).

over and reading them to my friends. All of us are getting really tired of Galatians. Why don't you translate the whole New Testament?"

I protested that it was impossible; I was a pastor — it had taken me two years to translate one of the smaller New Testament books. And besides, weren't there enough translations and paraphrases already? In the most recent definitive history of the Bible in English, David Daniell calculates that over twelve hundred new translations into English of the Bible, or parts of it, were made from the original Hebrew and Greek between 1945 and 1990. Thirty-five were fresh translations of the whole Bible, and eighty were fresh translations of the New Testament alone. His comment, "these are huge figures," is a huge understatement.[14]

My editor persisted. After a couple of years of letters and telephone conversations, it seemed "good to the Holy Spirit and to us" (editor and publisher, my wife and me) that this was the work set before us. I resigned from my congregation (after twenty-nine years) and set to work translating the biblical text into an American English vernacular.

When I sat down with the Hebrew and Greek texts to translate them into American for the congregation beyond my congregation, it didn't seem all that different from what I had been doing for thirty-five years as a pastor, a life ordained by my church to bring the word of God in Scripture and sacrament to the people whom I had been called to assist and guide into a life of worshipping God the Father, following Jesus the Son, and receiving the Holy Spirit in all the details involved in raising families and working for a living, living a joyful and responsible life in the American neighborhood. I was always aware as a pastor that I was required to be neighborhood-specific. Generalities and "big" truths would not do. My neighborhood was American; in *The Message* the language was necessarily American. I set to work. It would take me ten years.

14. David Daniell, *The Bible in English: Its History and Influence* (New Haven: Yale University Press, 2003), pp. 764-65.

CHAPTER 9

The Message

Language is sacred at its core. It has its origin in God. "In the beginning was the Word, and the Word was with God, and the Word was God" (John 1:1). When St. John rewrote Genesis, emphasizing the primacy of language (Word and words) in the very being-ness of God and the way God works, he went on to make the truly astonishing statement that "the Word became flesh and lived among us . . ." (John 1:14 NRSV). With that statement St. John launched his detailed witness of Jesus as that Word, Jesus revealing who he is (who *God* is), Jesus using the Aramaic language, the local street language of his day, to do it, to reveal God, the Word that was God in the beginning. When John wrote his witness, his Gospel, he translated the words and stories that he had heard Jesus speak in Aramaic into Greek. This Word, this Jesus, did not walk the roads of Palestine stopping off in villages to give lectures on divinity in the abstract, or post rules in the public squares on conduct acceptable to God, or explain the way things are in order to satisfy our natural curiosity. He both was the language and spoke the language that reveals God not from the outside but from the inside, God's heart, God's comprehensive way of being personally and relationally with us as Father, Son, and Holy Spirit. And the people understood him — "the common people heard him gladly" (Mark 12:37 ASV). He spoke the language of God in their language. As men and women received these words, they were *formed* by them into a "new creation," they were "born again."

This revelatory quality of language maintains its sacred creation and salvation core as we human beings continue to speak and listen to it, but especially as we use language to reveal to one another who we uniquely are. We are not just using words to exchange information — asking directions for making it across the street, getting or giving goods and services, identifying the red-tailed hawk and the fringed gentian, but *revealing ourselves:* revealing our hopes and dreams, our thoughts and prayers, that vast interiority that we summarize as *soul,* this unfathomable mystery of who we are as "image of God."

This sacredness of language, whether spoken or written, is liable to sacrilege in two directions, downward and upward. Sacrilege downward takes the form of blasphemy, language used to defile and desecrate. The sacredness of language inheres in its capacity to reveal what cannot be weighed and measured, its capacity to reveal spirit, interior reality, whether divine or human. If it is debased into cant or cliché or mendacity it violates the sacred essence of a man or woman — or God. It reduces reality, whether human or divine, to something less, something impersonal, a thing or an image that I can manipulate and use. Such language takes the attitude that if I have to be an anthill there aren't going to be any mountains.

Sacrilege upward takes place when language is inflated into balloons of abstraction or diffused into the insubstantiality of lacey gossamer. Pretentious language is as much a violation of the sacred core of language as blasphemy and cant. This happens when we use language to flatter or impress, when we use words to distance ourselves from relationship with others, whether the others are the persons of the Trinity or our parents, leaders, celebrities, friends, and neighbors. If we use language to set others on pedestals or install them in roles, we no longer have to deal with them as persons but only as ideas or representatives or functions. It sounds as if we are honoring them; in fact we are using language to keep them out of the neighborhoods in which we live our ordinary lives. We are then free to deal with them in escapist fantasies, in condescending criticism, in avaricious dreaming, or in curt dismissal. This is the desecration of language "upward."

When it comes to reading and responding to Scripture the danger of violations upward is much greater than that of violations downward for the simple reason that it is more difficult to detect. Outright blasphemy — an angry "God dammit!" — calls more attention to itself than obsequious piety — for example, "precious and exalted, holy and incomparable God Almighty . . ." intoned in a quavering voice. Ironically, the latter may be more a desecration of language than the former.

We seldom if ever think of it, but it doesn't take much imagination to realize that the first people who read the Bible didn't know they were reading the Bible. They were simply listening to stories of their ancestors Abraham and Samuel, or reading notes from old sermons written on scraps of paper, or discussing a letter from a man whom they had never heard of but some friends had told them was well worth listening to. These words carried no external authority with them. If the readers judged the "book by its cover," they could very easily be unimpressed, even scornful. The danger for them was sacrilege downward, despising what they didn't understand or reducing revelational intimacies to the latest in pious gossip. But it didn't take long for some of them to realize that these words revealed something about God that they could never have guessed, and gave them a language by which they could respond appropriately, answering from their hearts. The words were collected and honored; they became the text by which Christians lived their lives. That was a good thing; that is how we got our Bible.

But along the way the dangers of sacrilege shifted from downward to upward. Once the Bible became a revered authority it became possible to treat it as a thing, an impersonal authority, to use it to define or damn others, and to avoid dealing with God's word in a personal, relational, and obedient way. It didn't take long for people to start using the Bible as a cover, as a front, by honoring it, praising it as a verbal artifact, defending it as the Truth against all comers, treating it as a classic, as great literature, rather than receiving these words and responding to these words as God's word to them, personally. But the words of Scripture are not primarily words, however impressive, that label or define or prove, but words that mean, that reveal, that shape the soul, that generate saved lives, that form believing and obedient lives. Impersonal, opinionated, propagandizing, manipulating words, no matter how ardent and accurate, inflate upward. They lose rootage in hearts. They lose grounding in human dailiness. They are no longer at the service of listening and responding to the word, those words that reveal God's will and presence, the language in which we are invited to likewise reveal ourselves in prayer and praise, in obedience and love. *Having* and *defending* and *celebrating* the Bible instead of *receiving, submitting to,* and *praying* the Bible, masks an enormous amount of nonreading.

For those of us who take the Scriptures seriously as the word of God and the authoritative text by which we choose to live, translation is one of the primary defenses that we have against sacrilege upward, against letting language inflate into pomposities or artifices that are no longer current with the way we express our ordinary lives. And because pomposities are always "crouching at the door" of language, translators need to be on call to keep language from losing resonance with the common speech that we use when we talk with our children and friends. When the language in question is the Scriptures, the language God uses to reveal himself to us, the stakes are immense.

The most widely distributed and influential translation of the Bible in the English language was authorized by King James of England and published in 1611, the translation that continues to carry his name: the King James Version. This grand achievement, "the great monument of English and North American Protestantism,"[1] has benefited from a series of revisions based on the recovery of earlier and more accurate manuscripts.[2] But even though the revisions have provided us with an

1. Adam Nicolson, *God's Secretaries* (New York: HarperCollins, 2003), p. 188.
2. Revisions were made in 1881 (RV) and 1901 (ASV). The RSV in 1954 and the NRSV in 1989 continued in the Tyndale-KJV tradition but also became more and more independent versions in their own right as they were increasingly concerned with dealing with antiquated language.

impressively accurate text, they have not prevented a continuously widening gap between the language of the Bible and the language we use in our everyday lives.

But then, in 1897 and later in 1923, archaeological discoveries were made that infused fresh blood into Bible translations. Translators went to work on the text with impressive results. The village of Oxyrhynchus in Egypt and the ancient kingdom of Ugarit in Syria were the sites where these discoveries took place, discoveries that introduced a completely new dimension into the post–King James world of Bible translation. The two place names are not exactly household words among Bible readers but they should be, for between them they bring into view a world of language and culture that has revolutionized (not too strong a word, I think) the translation of the Bible.

Oxyrhynchus and Ugarit

Oxyrhynchus is in Egypt. Egypt has always been the darling of archaeologists, courted by virtually everyone interested in the ancient world. A world of wonders: the Giza pyramids, the inscrutable sphinx, the Karnak temple, the brobdingnagian statues, the high art of hieroglyphics. A place of marvels to behold and mysteries to solve. But the discovery that did far more to affect the Christian mind than all the previous Egyptian marvels and mysteries put together was made in a village garbage dump at Oxyrhynchus on the Nile, 160 miles south of Cairo. Oxyrhynchus boasted no temples, no pyramid tombs, no statues of Horus and Osiris, nothing worth photographing, nothing worth hiring a camel to go and see. Just that garbage dump where a couple of men unearthed some scraps of paper, the discarded contents of the town's wastebaskets. The men were British, Bernard Grenfell and Arthur Hunt. The year was 1897. The scraps of paper (papyri) they unearthed from that garbage dump had Greek writing on them. From the moment that Grenfell and Hunt read the first words on these discarded pieces of paper, they knew they were in on something big, *very* big. "Epoch-making," the phrase used by the American Lutheran lexicographers William Arndt and Wilfred Gingrich to describe the discoveries, errs, if anything, on the side of understatement.[3]

As already noted, in the world in which the twenty-seven documents that compose our New Testament were written, Greek was the prevailing language. Much as Aramaic had been the *lingua franca* of the Persian empire, Greek was the unifying language of the Greek and Roman empires that succeeded it. Regardless of your cradle language — Egyptian, Latin, Syriac, Arabic — if you had been alive in the age ushered in by Alexander the Great, a great missionary for all things Greek, you would have spoken some Greek. If newspapers had been published in those years, they would have been in Greek. Business was conducted in Greek, government decrees were issued in Greek, school subjects were learned in Greek. Not everywhere, of course, for local languages also persisted, but mostly.

At the time that Jesus was born in Bethlehem, Greek was already an ancient language — at least a thousand years of writings that made up an impressive library of literature: Homer and Xenophon, Pindar and Aeschylus, Sappho and Euclid, Heraclitus and Parmenides, Plato and Aristotle. Great epics, spellbinding drama, penetrating history, lyrical poetry, profound philosophy, clear-sighted science. This Greek was a resilient, elegant, and supple language capable of immense subtleties.

Around 500 B.C. the dialect of Athens (Attic Greek) had emerged as the dominant Greek of the area and imposed itself on the several dialects of the Greek homelands; it became the common dialect, the common vehicle for communication, especially in business affairs and military expeditions. It was also this Attic Greek that gained enormous status as a literary language in the classical period (500 to 323 B.C.). But at the time of Alexander the Great's military and cultural conquests of all the countries from Greece to India and from Syria to Egypt, as Greek developed into the common language across this vast, many-

3. *A Greek-English Lexicon of the New Testament and Other Early Christian Literature*, third English ed., revised and edited by Frederick William Danker (Chicago: University of Chicago Press, 2000), p. v.

languaged territory, it lost a good bit of its elegance. As it was adapted to international usage — military, mercantile, diplomatic — the gap between where this Greek began (preserved in Attic classical literature) and where it ended up (the language of the people) became significant. The Attic dialect of Athens thus evolved into what we customarily refer to as the *Koine* or "common" Greek of the Hellenistic period and of the New Testament. Meanwhile, philosophers, poets, dramatists, and historians continued to write in classical Greek, "proper" Greek. All students learned that serious writers must shun the common *(koine)* language, which was fit only for nonliterary use.

The consequence was that in the course of the three centuries preceding Jesus and the formation of the Christian church, there were two levels of Greek language: the classical Greek represented by the great writers of the past, and the common Greek in use across the empire to conduct all the affairs of everyday life. If you intended to write history or philosophy or poetry, you would use the best Greek available, classical Greek. But if you were carrying on a conversation with your neighbors or shopping in the market, you would use the Koine, the common tongue. If from time to time you supplemented your conversation with writing, this nonliterary writing found its way into a wastebasket and from there eventually to the garbage dump.

So here's the thing: Only what was written in classical Greek survived, the writings that ended up in libraries and government archives, or on monuments and in formal inscriptions — the kind of writing that professional writers, "real" writers, wrote.

Time passed. The documents that became our New Testament were gathered and honored. Eventually they were wedded to the Greek translation of the Hebrew Scriptures (the Septuagint) and became the text for the Christian church — authoritative as the word of God. As the Roman Empire extended its range and influence they were, bit by bit, translated into Latin. The translators, of course, noticed that the Greek of Paul and Mark was quite different from the Greek they had learned in the schools. The Greek of the New Testament sounded so barbarous to the educated that it had to be defended by the early church. Over the centuries of translation two theories emerged to account for the oddity of New Testament Greek as compared to classical Greek. One group thought that New Testament Greek must have been a translation from an original Hebrew text. These were the "Hebraists": they argued that an underlying Hebrew original accounted for the un-Greek quality of the writing. The other group — these were the "purists" — conjectured that New Testament Greek was a special language, created by the Holy Spirit to suit the purposes of God's revelation. The classical Greek that provided the base was purified of its pagan origins by the refining fire of the Spirit.

The Greek New Testament has a vocabulary of about five thousand words. Of those five thousand words, about five hundred were considered unique to the New Testament, never appearing in any extant secular Greek literature up to that point. The "purists" seized on this statistic to suggest that the Spirit modified the secular Greek to give it a distinctive "Holy Spirit" cast, and then seeded it with freshly coined "Holy Spirit" words to confirm its exalted status as the language of revelation. Just as the Holy Ghost inspired the writers, Mark and Luke, Paul and John and the others, he also supplied the special words necessary to convey the uniqueness of the message. This language, "biblical Greek," was exclusive to the Bible and never profaned by common use. A German theologian, Richard Rothe, went so far as to call it the "language of the Holy Ghost."[4]

There was never any question but that New Testament Greek was different from classical Greek. But how to account for the difference? The "Hebraists" and the "purists," in their quite different ways, did their best to come up with an answer.

Until that April day in 1897 when Bernard Grenfell and Arthur Hunt fished that first piece of paper out of the Oxyrhynchus rubbish heap. And then another and then another. As they read these they were able to piece together what life was like on the muddy streets, crowded markets, and noisy playgrounds of ancient Alexandria. Early on they noticed that many of the words they were reading were among the five

4. In James Hope Moulton, *A Grammar of New Testament Greek*, 4 vols., third ed. (Edinburgh: T. & T. Clark, 1908), vol. 1 (*Prolegomena*), p. 3.

hundred or so Holy Ghost words that were supposedly unique to the New Testament. As they continued to decipher and read what was written on these unimposing scraps of papyrus paper they were able to account for nearly all five hundred words. The words came from wills, official reports, letters from husbands away on business to their wives at home, a letter that a son who had become a soldier wrote to his parents, a letter in which a father admonished his children who were away from home, petitions, accounts, shopping lists, bills and receipts — the kinds of writings that never get bound into books and catalogued in a library. This was the kind of writing that, when it has done its work, is thrown away. Scholars and translators working on the Bible had no idea that this language was even there for the very good reason that it had never come within throwing distance of a library — these casual, "unliterary" writings had all been buried in the garbage dumps. All those special words that occurred nowhere else in written records, those "Holy Ghost" words, were all the time buried in a town garbage dump, preserved under Egyptian sand. They were all street words, spontaneous, unstudied expressions out of the immediacy of workplace and kitchen.

The scholars who now went to work on these unpretentious scraps of paper would completely reorient the presuppositions of biblical translators. A young German professor, Adolf Deissmann, was the pioneer. He carefully assessed each new word, studied its context, and worked at understanding and appreciating the kind of language God uses as he makes himself known among us.[5] He was followed up by the great English Greek scholar James Hope Moulton, who immediately went to work rewriting the definitive grammar of New Testament Greek by using the new evidence from the scraps of paper, the "papyri." Summing up the impact of what he was doing he wrote:

The New Testament writers had little idea that they were writing literature [otherwise they would have written in literary Greek].

5. He tells the story in fascinating detail in his *Light from the Ancient East*, trans. Lionel Strachan, fourth ed. (New York: George H. Doran, 1927; first ed., 1910).

The Holy Ghost spoke absolutely in the language of the people, as we might surely have expected He would. . . . The very grammar and dictionary cry out against men who would allow the Scriptures to appear in any other form than that "understanded of the people."[6]

A half-century later, Professor C. F. D. Moule weighed in with his assessment: "The arrival of papyrus fragments from Egypt upon the philologists' desks marks a new area in the study of New Testament Greek."[7]

A generation before these discoveries were made — discoveries that absolutely revolutionized biblical translation — Bishop Lightfoot, one of England's most insightful New Testament scholars, in a prescient aside while lecturing, said, "if we could only recover letters that ordinary people wrote to each other without any thought of being literary, we should have the greatest possible help for understanding of the language of the New Testament generally."[8] Well, they were discovered — and what a help they have been!

The difference that this has made to Bible translation and Bible reading is hard to exaggerate. In retrospect it shouldn't have been such a surprise that this was the kind of language used in the Bible, for this is exactly the kind of society that we know that Jesus embraced and loved, the world of children and marginal men and women, the rough-talking working class, the world of the poor and dispossessed and exploited. Still, it was a surprise: our Bibles written not in the educated and polished language of scholars, historians, philosophers, and theologians but in the common language of fishermen and prostitutes, homemakers and carpenters. Not entirely, to be sure. F. F. Bruce cautions against exaggerating the extent to which the Greek vernacular is taken over wholesale into the Greek New Testament. There are wide

6. Moulton, *Grammar*, p. 5.

7. C. F. D. Moule, *An Idiom-Book of New Testament Greek* (Cambridge: Cambridge University Press, 1959), p. 3.

8. Quoted by Moulton, *Grammar*, p. 242.

differences in style within the New Testament, ranging from true literary works (Hebrews and First Peter) to the vernacular conversation of ordinary people (the Gospels), with Paul coming roughly halfway between.[9] But now that it is all laid out before us, it makes perfect sense. Of course the witnesses of God's revelation to us would use the language most accessible to us. Professor Moulton had it right: "The Holy Ghost spoke absolutely in the language of the people, as we might surely have expected He would."

Two representative examples. An adjective appears in the Lord's Prayer, the word usually translated "daily," for which there is no precedent in classical Greek (Matt. 6:11 and Luke 11:3). It would be hard to find a more striking instance of a "Holy Ghost" word: "Give us this day our *daily* bread." In Greek *epiousion*. So what kind of bread are we to pray for?

One commentator on the Sermon on the Mount targets the fourth petition of the Lord's Prayer as its most famous crux: "the most controversial and difficult of the petitions."[10] So much hangs on the proper translation of *ton arton ton epiousion,* which is usually (and properly) translated "daily bread."

So why is this petition a crux? Because if we get this one wrong, the entire prayer is undermined, or at the very least skewed. This is the only petition that deals with materiality. The Prayer has six petitions: the first three pray for the furtherance of God and his work — his holiness, his will, his kingdom; the matching triad is oriented around human needs — food, forgiveness, deliverance. The pair of triads is connected by the phrase, "on earth as it is in heaven," which is to say that prayer has its source in heaven, the home country, so to speak, of God, but the action takes place on earth — *our* home country. Prayer that is not firmly grounded "on earth" is not prayer as our Lord taught us to pray.

9. F. F. Bruce, *The Books and the Parchments,* revised ed. (London: Marshall Pickering, 1991), p. 55.

10. Dale C. Allison, *The Sermon on the Mount: Inspiring the Moral Imagination* (New York: Crossroad, 1999), p. 125.

The petition immediately following the "on earth" formula is the petition for bread, as if to underline the earthiness of the entire prayer. Bread is unique among the six items prayed for in that it is the only one that is unavoidably physical, material, something that we can touch and taste, that enters into our bodily functions. All the others — God's holiness, will, and kingdom, our forgiveness of sin and deliverance from evil — are "spiritual" and not subject to examination in a laboratory. And so they are also vulnerable to "spiritualization," the understanding and interpreting of them in unearthly ways. But not bread. We are physically involved with bread, whether in its making or purchase or eating. We can't go to the market and buy God's holiness, will, or kingdom, or our forgiveness or deliverance. But we can bread. We can't knead and bake, butter and eat the holiness, will, and kingdom of God, nor our forgiveness of sin and deliverance from evil. But we can bread. Bread stubbornly resists spiritualization. We can't spiritualize bread.

Or can we?

Most readers of Matthew and Luke when they come to the fourth petition, even though they don't know the precise meaning of *epiousion,* read it in the plain sense: *daily* bread, bread *for the day,* enough to eat. But a considerable number of men and women, more often than not from the company of biblical scholars and theologians, have not read it that way. *Epiousion,* because it could not be defined from the dictionary or other usage, seemed to provide an open invitation to reinterpret plain ordinary bread into something quite different, some kind of "spiritual" bread. *Epiousion,* after all, was one of the "Bible words." And occurring right at the center of the Lord's Prayer, it must, it was assumed, have a deeper "spiritual" meaning consistent with and maybe even exceeding the spirituality of the other five petitions, a "Holy Ghost" meaning.

The unique word proved irresistible to reinterpretation by devout scholars and they went to work on it with great zest almost immediately, "spiritualizing" bread in various ways. We find instances as early as the second century A.D. It was common in the early church to completely suppress the petition as a request for actual bread. It must be

something very special to get a special adjective all to itself. Some suggested the Bread of Life; others the Lord's Supper (Eucharist), miracle
manna, the Messianic banquet. Lancelot Andrewes, the leader of the
King James translators, taking his cue from Psalm 78:25, came up with
"angel's food." Origen, writing in Alexandria in the third century, a
scholar and theologian of immense learning, served up the most "spiritual" suggestion of all, *supersubstantial bread*. But Origen was a man ill
at ease with his own body; in order to keep his mind concentrated
without distraction on the things of God he had himself castrated. In
his homily *On Prayer*, his exposition of the Lord's Prayer, he goes on at
great length, first remarking on the absence of the word *epiousion*
(daily) in any Greek writing known to him and then speculating on
what must have been its very special spiritual meaning. It didn't seem
plausible to someone of Origen's mind-set to imagine that Jesus would
teach us to pray for a plain loaf of pumpernickel made of flour and
yeast and baked in an oven. He must mean bread that is beyond mere
bread. Origen is unambiguous and emphatic: "the bread for which we
should ask is spiritual . . . 'the living bread that comes down from
heaven.'"[11]

Seventeen hundred years after Origen, Albert Debrunner, a professor at the University of Bern, was going over some of the Oxyrhynchus scraps of wastepaper at his library worktable and discovered
the very word, *epiousion*, in an ancient housekeeping book, a shopping
list that also included chickpeas and straw.[12] In 1914, eleven years before Debrunner published his findings, Adolf Deissmann, without specific evidence, had speculated that *epiousion* "had the appearance of a
word that originated in the trade and traffic of the everyday life of the
people."[13] With the Oxyrhynchus scrap of paper before him, Debrunner confirmed it.

And there it stands: perhaps at the very moment that Jesus was

11. *Origen: On Prayer*, trans. Rowan A. Greer (New York: Paulist, 1979), p. 141.
12. Werner Foerster in *Theological Dictionary of the New Testament*, ed. G. Kittel,
trans. G. W. Bromiley (Grand Rapids: Eerdmans, 1964), vol. 2, p. 591.
13. Deissmann, *Light from the Ancient East*, p. 78.

on a Galilean hillside teaching his disciples to pray for daily bread (*arton epiousion* — or their Aramaic equivalent), down in Egypt a mother was writing out a shopping list for her teenage son as she sent him off to market, emphasizing that the bread was to be fresh, *today's* bread — "Don't let that baker sell you any stale, day-old bread, make sure it's fresh (*epiousion*) bread!"

In retrospect we can reconstruct this scenario: Origen, honored still today as one of the most learned of all the biblical scholars that the church has ever had, wrote out his interpretation of the fourth petition of the Lord's Prayer, assembling page after page of evidence (nine and a half pages in my English translation) demonstrating that it is unthinkable that Jesus would instruct us to pray for anything remotely suggesting the bread that we toast and butter and eat with our morning coffee. And all the while he was at his desk, writing devoutly and learnedly, the very word that he was taking such pains to de-materialize was buried a couple of hundred miles south in that village garbage dump just west of the Nile River. There it was, this unpretentious adjective quietly waiting to make its appearance and insist on the so frequently overlooked obvious, that bread, fresh-baked, yeast-fragrant, crisp-crusted bread is the pivotal petition in the Lord's Prayer, pivotal for keeping "on earth as it is in heaven" as the firm foundation for our prayed obedience in following Jesus.

Hans Dieter Betz, in his magisterial commentary on the Sermon on the Mount, after comprehensively reviewing every attempt to spiritualize the bread that Jesus commanded us to pray for, doesn't buy it — despite the authority of Origen and his considerable progeny. His conclusion: "There is hardly any doubt that [Jesus] refers to real, not merely 'spiritual' bread. . . ."[14]

Another example. Near the end of First Peter, Jesus is referred to as the "chief Shepherd" of our souls (5:3). "Chief shepherd" was one of those five hundred "biblical words" with no known occurrence in secular us-

---

14. Hans Dieter Betz, *The Sermon on the Mount* (Minneapolis: Fortress, 1995), p. 399.

age, a word looking very much as if it had been newly coined by Peter especially for Jesus. Jesus had, after all, referred to himself as the good shepherd (John 10:11). What could be more fitting for Peter than to raise the "good" to a higher level, to "chief." The term "chief shepherd" is a compound word, a combination of *archē*, chief, and *poimēn*, shepherd, producing *archipoimēn*, chief shepherd. It makes perfect sense in the context of Peter's letter to read it as an exalted title: Jesus, the chief shepherd, the shepherd of all shepherds, a superlative after the manner of "King of kings and Lord of lords" (Rev. 19:16). And then the word was found in an Egyptian garbage dump, written this time not on a piece of paper but on a slip of wood hung around the neck of an Egyptian mummy, a kind of dog tag, identifying the corpse. There was a grammatical mistake in the labeling, evidence that it was written hurriedly by someone not well-educated. And its presence in a garbage dump was evidence that the family and friends couldn't afford a decent burial — a far cry from the opulent pyramid tombs for which Egypt is so famous! No, this was an Egyptian peasant who had been the overseer of two or three other shepherds, an *archipoimēn*, what we would probably designate as a straw boss, or, at most, a crew foreman.[15] Contrary to exalting Jesus above the common herd, Peter used a word that put Jesus in the company of working-class peasants and cheap burials. And what else would we expect, knowing Jesus' embrace of the "poorest of the poor" and his identification with the despised and the weak.

The discoveries made at Oxyrhynchus and other Egyptian sites are irrefutable evidence that the language of our New Testament is primarily the language of the street (although, as noted earlier, not entirely). Why should this surprise anyone? But it invariably does. When Augustine first read the Bible he was greatly disappointed. As Peter Brown explains,

> He had grown up expecting a book to be cultivated and polished: he had been carefully groomed to communicate with educated men in the only admissible way, in a Latin scrupulously modeled

15. Deissmann, *Light from the Ancient East*, p. 100.

on the ancient authors. Slang and jargon were equally abhorrent to such a man; and the Latin Bible of Africa, translated some centuries before by humble, nameless writers, was full of both. What is more, what Augustine read in the Bible seemed to have little to do with the highly spiritual Wisdom that Cicero had told him to love. It was cluttered with earthy and immoral stories from the Old Testament; and, even in the New Testament, Christ, Wisdom Himself, was introduced by long, and contradictory, genealogies.[16]

It was only after his conversion that he realized that this word of God was not an elevated language used by philosophers and poets to discourse on the "higher things" but the language in which men and women were finding themselves addressed by the Holy Spirit in the thick of everyday life.

Not unlike Augustine, we often thoughtlessly suppose that language dealing with a holy God and holy things should be stately, elevated, and ceremonial. But it is a supposition that won't survive the scrutiny of one good look at Jesus — his preference for homely stories and his easy association with common people, his birth in a stable and his death on cross. For Jesus is the *descent* of God to our lives just as we are and in the neighborhoods in which we live, not the *ascent* of our lives to God whom we hope will approve when he sees how hard we try and how politely we pray.

And Ugarit in Syria. Oxyrhynchus was an immersion in biblical language, a street language that no one in the first century would have dreamed of using when writing anything serious, the same kind of language that we use when we are exasperated with our children or buying a used car. The discoveries made in the excavations of Ugarit had a different impact. Ugarit provided an immersion in the culture within which the biblical faith was formed — and what a culture it was! The promised land into which God led our fathers and mothers was, fa-

16. Peter Brown, *Augustine of Hippo* (Berkeley: University of California Press, 1969), p. 42.

mously, "flowing with milk and honey." But it was also, the Ugaritic evidence shows, flowing with violence and sex and magic.

Thirty years after the Oxyrhynchus wastebaskets were unearthed and sorted through in Egypt, a farmer in Syria working his field plowed into a burial tomb. The tomb turned out to be the tip of a glacier, the ancient kingdom of Ugarit, buried under three thousand years of Syrian sand. Within a year or two a team of French archaeologists had gathered thousands of baked clay tablets inscribed in an unknown cuneiform alphabet and in an unknown language. It wasn't long before both script and language were deciphered. The language turned out to be very much like biblical Hebrew. The clay tablets provided a detailed accounting of the culture that the Hebrews encountered and were immersed in upon arriving in Canaan after their long stint of Egyptian slavery. One of the men who figured out the alphabet and language of Ugarit had learned his trade from years spent cracking enemy secret codes during World War I, a nice juxtaposition of ancient and contemporary!

As tablet after tablet was translated, a whole world gradually opened up, the world that the Hebrews inhabited when they entered "the promised land." At the time, Israel was a people still in formation. In many fundamental ways they didn't "fit" into the culture and politics of Canaan. Canaan was made up of city-states, each ruled by its own king; Israel was loosely organized by tribes, each with its own tradition and identity. When necessary, a "judge" would emerge to take care of whatever crisis faced the people at the time. Loosely organized as they were, they didn't get along with one another very well. They were an embryonic people of God still, in formation as the People of God. But Canaan and the culture of Canaan was now their home and would be for several hundred years.

Previous to discovering the kingdom of Ugarit and its huge library, we knew Canaan — the country in which Israel lived and worshipped, believed and rebelled, sang songs and preached sermons — only from the outside, that is, from what we could pick up from allusions and references embedded in the Hebrew Bible. For the most part Israel's Scriptures portrayed Canaanite culture as the enemy: hostile, pagan, and a powerful and unrelenting source of seduction away from the life of salvation and faith to go "whoring" (the crude but bluntly accurate verb used by the Hebrew prophets) after the "other gods" of Canaan, of which, it turns out, they had a great number and variety to choose from.

None of this cultural information was absolutely new. For two hundred years our scholars had been learning a great deal about the world in which the biblical story was formed as the languages, religions, and politics of Mesopotamia and Egypt came to light. We knew where the Hebrews had come from and a great deal about their surrounding cultures. But we never knew much about their next-door neighbors, the people they rubbed shoulders with as they were being formed into a people of God. Ugarit provided that, sharpening our understanding and appreciation of how Israel managed to both survive and maintain its identity "in but not of" the culture of Canaan.[17]

Two things coming out of the Ugarit explorations are of particular interest in terms of Bible translation. One is that Israel shared the Canaanite language and culture without being overpowered by it. The other is that while they used similar literary forms, the content was radically different: Israel faithfully wrote the family stories of their ancestors, in contrast to the Canaanites, who invented fanciful myths about gods.

Take culture and language. Israel used the language of Canaan, wrote its poetry in the style and rhythms of Canaan, used the god-words of Canaan. But they took the culture of Canaan and used it to make something distinctively and uniquely their own — which is to say that the culture of Israel doesn't come to us in a pure state, a culture uncontaminated by the sex-and-religion paganism of Canaan. The scriptural revelation and life of salvation did not develop in isolation from their Canaanite neighbors.

For instance, *El*, the regular Canaanite term for god, was also a

17. See G. Ernest Wright, *The Old Testament against Its Environment* (Chicago: Alec R. Allenson, 1950).

term freely used by the Hebrews. Among the Canaanites *El* was the head god, the father of the gods, who with his wife Asherah fathered a vast progeny of gods and goddesses. The Hebrews seemed unembarrassed to share the word, tainted as it was, with their neighbors. Likewise, there were colorful phrases that the Canaanites used in relation to their gods that the Hebrews picked up from old myths and used freely in prayers to their God: *rider of the clouds* (cf. Ps. 68:4), *you broke the heads of the dragons in the waters. You crushed the heads of Leviathan* (Ps. 74:13-14). Psalm 29 and other psalms display close parallels in terminology with Canaanite poems discovered at Ugarit. Perhaps even more significant than the taking over of Canaanite god-words and phrases is that Israel also took over the Ugaritic forms of poetry. Much of the Hebrew Bible is written in poetry, and the Hebrews were magnificent poets. As the translated cuneiform tablets accumulated, it became clear that the Hebrews had learned much of their craft of poetry from their Canaanite neighbors. One of the glories of the Hebrew Bible, its skillfully employed poetic forms and rhythms used to the glory of God, turns out to be a hand-me-down from pagan Canaan.

But while the Hebrews were perfectly at home in Canaanite culture in one sense, willing and able to use the language and adapt its forms, they were also practiced in discernment. They knew how to say "no" to the culture when they had to. This becomes clear when we realize that in a culture that celebrated many gods, Israel was fiercely loyal to one God, represented throughout the Old Testament as a "jealous" God. The prohibition "Thou shalt not make unto thee any graven image" (Exod. 20:4 KJV) was absolutely unique in that world — there was nothing like it in the whole ancient Middle East. The Canaanites carried out an assembly line industry in god-images, but not a single figure of a male deity has yet been found in the debris of any Israelite town. On the other hand, a great number of mother-goddess figurines are found in every excavation of Israelite houses, which indicates that at a popular level it was common to verge dangerously near to polytheism. But one of our best interpreters of this archaeological evidence, George Ernest Wright, conjectures that people had the female figurines in their homes "not so much for theological as for magical reasons, using them as 'good luck' charms,"[18] much as a rabbit's foot or a Christopher medal shows up casually among us without any sense of the second commandment being violated. And it is significant that in a culture that was saturated with female goddesses the Hebrews did not even have a word for "goddess" — even though their neighbors held female divinities in the highest regard. As far as Israel was concerned there was nothing to them — not even a word for them!

Moreover, a sharp line was drawn against all magical practices. Canaan was full of magic, technologies designed to manipulate the gods and goddesses to perform favors. Israel was adamant in its rejection of anything that so much as hinted at magical religious technology — God is not at our service, we are at God's service. The Mosaic commandment not to boil a kid in its mother's milk (Exod. 23:19 and 34:26), sitting on the page as it does completely without context, has puzzled Bible readers no end. Judaism later did the best it could to take this text seriously by developing a kosher dietary system that insisted on a strict separation of dairy and meat products. But it is possible (but by no means certain) that the text may turn out to be an abrupt, one-liner rejection of anything that smacked of magical practice. A Ugaritic cuneiform tablet that deals with a magic spell cast by means of milk may indicate that the Mosaic prohibition in essence says, "Stay clear of all the Canaanite magic spells and rituals! Your job is to worship God, not wheedle him."[19]

And stories. The other aspect of the Ugaritic discoveries that illuminates the way we translate and read our Scriptures has to do with the Canaanite fondness for myth-making. A myth, in contrast to a story, is cut loose from history and without rootage in the world that we live in; it is a tale about the gods in settings that do not include us. We are spectators at best — the gods operate in a world of their own. All the real action takes place between gods and goddesses. As it turns out, most

18. George Ernest Wright, *Biblical Archaeology* (Philadelphia: Westminster, 1957), p. 117.

19. See Gerhard von Rad, *Old Testament Theology*, vol. 1 (New York: Harper and Brothers, 1962), p. 27.

of the action has to do with fighting and copulating. Violence and sex keep the action going. The myths of Canaan are no different in this respect from those everywhere else in that world; what is new for us is the realization that these myths are the stock-in-trade of Israel's neighbors, the people who lived across the street, the merchants they haggled with at the market. Canaanite religion was all about gods and their adventures. If you wanted in on it you engaged in magical manipulations — impersonal, nonrelational, acquisitive religious technologies. While their Canaanite neighbors were elaborating their wonderful myths of sky gods, thunder gods, and fertility gods and goddesses off somewhere in the far north, Israel was telling stories of their ancestors whose names they knew and in whose land they lived, ancestors who listened to and understood God present and personal to them in their everyday lives. God was present and active among them. Local and ancestral history, not legendary mythic worlds, was where they learned to deal with God. Their stories were rooted in the family history of their parents and grandparents. By implication, they were included.

Myths are a way to create an imaginative world in which we can visualize the gods, put them on stage and see them at work, and then, by employing magical rituals and incantations, try to get them to work for us. It is all out in the open; there is no mystery. Neither is there any personal relationship — the gods couldn't care less about us; our only recourse is to bribe or manipulate them in some way or other. You may know the names of the gods and goddesses, but they don't know yours. Stories, in contrast, are restrained, respecting the reclusiveness and silence of God, letting God work and be in God's own way, respecting the essential mystery of his being and trusting his goodness and providence in our lives.

Baal is the most colorful god by far in the Canaanite mythology and gets the most press.[20] Most of the action features blood and mayhem.

---

20. See James B. Pritchard, *Ancient Near Eastern Texts* (Princeton, N.J.: Princeton University Press, 1955), pp. 129-42; and Theodor H. Gaster, *Thespis: Ritual, Myth, and Drama in the Ancient Near East* (Garden City, N.Y.: Anchor, 1961), pp. 153-244.

In one scene Baal has a fight with two rival gods, Sir Sea (Yamm) and Sir River (Nahar). Sir Craft (Kothar), the god who makes things, brings Baal two magical clubs, Chaser (Yagrush) and Driver (Ayamur), to help him out. In the fight, Chaser turns out to be ineffective; Sea and River get knocked around a good bit but not knocked out. Then Baal grabs Driver, the second club; the magic kicks in and the rivals are vanquished. Just as Baal is about to finish them off, the mother goddess, Asherah (maybe Baal's mother or grandmother), steps in and restrains him: "What do you think you are doing? You have no business killing gods! Don't you have any sense?"

The gods are like schoolboys duking it out on the playground during recess. And then the school principal, a stern and sturdy woman, stops the mayhem, grabs them by their ears, and hauls them off to her office.

A companion myth features Baal's wife Anath on an occasion in which she goes on a rampage of vengeance against the henchmen of Baal's great rival Sir Death (Mot). The massacre takes place across a vast area from seacoast to sunrise. Heads roll like soccer balls across the ground. Severed hands fly up and fill the air like a swarm of locusts. Anath ties the heads between and around her breasts, hangs the hands from her waist, and strides through the bloodbath that she has created, up to her hips in gore. Then, as if that were not enough — her breasts resplendent with the bloody skulls and her hips festooned with the bloody hands — she fills a temple with men, locks the doors, and assaults them by hurling chairs and tables and footstools. Soon she is up to her knees in blood — no, up to her neck! "Her liver swelled with laughter; her heart full of joy." When all the killing was done, she became all feminine again. She got a basin of water and washed in the "dew of heaven," beautified herself with cosmetics — eyeshadow and rouge — and anointed herself with expensive perfume. Such a fine lady! She was, after all, the goddess of both love and war. The Egyptians, the pornographers of the Middle East, improved on the basic legend by portraying Anath provocatively naked on a galloping horse, brandishing shield and lance.

There are a lot more myths of the same sort. These are the myths that formed and filled the Canaanite imagination, ranging from the silly to the sordid (state-sponsored Ugaritic X-rated television).

Meanwhile, living in that same environment, sharing that identical culture and language, the Hebrews were telling stories, a narrative form far removed from myth. Only human beings make history, and all the history of the Hebrews was local, family history. The story of Abraham, Sarah, and the three strangers is representative (Gen. 18:1-15).

When three strangers show up at his tent one day, Abraham welcomes them and offers hospitality: Sarah makes fresh bread, Abraham runs off to get a calf and directs his servant to barbecue it. When all is ready, he sets out milk and curds and stands in attendance as his guests eat the sumptuous meal under the shade of oak trees. Then there is this conversation. The men ask Abraham, "Where is your wife, Sarah?" "Right there in the tent," says Abraham. One of the guests speaks, "I'll be back in a year and by the time I arrive, Sarah will have a son." Sarah, hiding behind the tent flap, is eavesdropping. When she hears that, she can't help herself; she laughs. She is an old woman, eighty years old; her husband is an old man, a hundred years old. A joke, certainly. Sarah laughs. Then the storyteller, without calling attention to what he is doing, identifies one of the guests as God, "the Lord." God proceeds to counter Sarah's levity with a solemn assertion, "Is anything too wonderful for the Lord?"

Where did the Hebrews learn to tell God-stories like this — spare, understated, embedded in the daily ordinary? Certainly not from the neighbors with whom they shared a common culture. In this story God enters into the lives of Abraham and Sarah anonymously and unobtrusively. The setting, the oak grove at Mamre, is unpretentious. The action is anchored in routine desert hospitality. The conversation is unadorned and matter-of-fact. Sarah is quite right, we feel, to laugh at what one of the men — only later identified without fanfare as God — says. And what God says without any rhetorical flourishes has to do with ordinary life — conception, pregnancy, birth. The "impossibility" regarding what is said, is absorbed in the ordinariness of what will take place. Israel's way of telling stories about God was not to write about God as such, but about God as he is present, often unnoticed, frequently anonymous, among actual men and women located in time and place, in the context of their ancestors and in the towns and valleys and mountains in which they had all grown up.

And there are a lot more stories of the same sort. These are the stories that formed Israel's imagination — quiet, everyday, the supernatural camouflaged in the natural, the presence of God revealed in the places and among the people involved in our day-to day-living. The entire biblical text stands in sturdy contrast to the myths of Ugarit — but also to the potpourri of religious psychology, self-development, mystical experimentation, and devotional dilettantism that provides the textual basis for so much contemporary religion.

Many people prefer to have their Bibles translated in the finest prose and poetry. It stands to reason: Language that deals with a holy God, holy ideas, and holy things ought to be an elevated language, stately and ceremonial. They want to keep the language of the Bible refined and, as far as possible, isolated from association with the sinful world. And they want it printed on India paper and bound handsomely in leather. It stands to reason: The culture in which God works requires protection from the noisy, contaminating world. A Bible ought to reflect a culture of reverence and majesty.

But the Holy Spirit will have little of that. The inspiration arrives in a rough, bumpy, and earthy language that reveals God's presence and action where we least expect it, catching us when we are up to our elbows in the soiled ordinariness of our culture (Ugarit!) and when spiritual thoughts are the farthest thing from our minds (Oxyrhynchus!). That is not to say that there is anything irreverent or flip in our Scriptures. And it is not to say that there are not splendid writers in our Bibles. There is an enormous sense of awe and respect and reverence in this Bible. Mystery is everywhere. The Holy is pervasive. But the surrounding culture is pagan, and much of the language from right off the street.

The greatest of the early translators of the Bible into English, William Tyndale (the first printing of his New Testament was published in

1526), somehow knew this long before the discovery of the Oxyrhynchus papyri and the Ugarit tablets. I think he knew it because he knew how the gospel worked, knew that the language of the message had to be congruent with the character and way of life of the Messenger. He said that he was translating so that "the boy that driveth the plough" would be able to read the Scriptures. He knew by gospel instinct what the papryi and tablets confirmed four hundred years later, that (as James Hope Moulton put it) "not only is the subject matter of the Scriptures unique but so also the language in which they came to be written or translated."[21] Tyndale did not mean a uniqueness provided by a special "Holy Ghost" language, as had once been thought, but saw the language of the Scriptures as being uniquely colloquial, the language of everyday. And Martin Luther, contemporary with Tyndale and grandfather of all Reformation translators (his New Testament was published in 1522), was adamant that when faced with translating the biblical text, "You've got to go out and ask the mother in her house, the children in the street, the ordinary man at the market. Watch their mouths move when they talk, and translate that way. Then they'll understand you and realize that you are speaking *German* to them."[22] The power of his translation of the Bible into German came as much from what he learned on the streets as from the work that he did in the library. To understand, for instance, the sacrificial rituals in the Mosaic law, he had the town butcher cut up sheep so he could study their entrails.[23]

But despite and in contrast to the pioneering and language-renewing colloquial translations of Luther in German and Tyndale in English, the King James translation with its smooth, majestic sonorities — an English least representative of the kind of language in which the Bible was first spoken and heard and written — continues after nearly four hundred years to be the most frequently purchased and widely distrib-

21. Moulton, *Grammar*, vol. 3 *(Syntax)*, p. 9.
22. Quoted in Nicolson, *God's Secretaries*, p. 185.
23. Henry Zecher, "How One Man's Pen Changed the World," *Christianity Today* (October 2, 1983).

uted translation in the English-speaking world. The King James translators used Tyndale's text as their baseline, taking over approximately three-quarters of it essentially unchanged.[24] But what they did with that plagiarized text amounted to a violation of it — they put lace cuffs on Tyndale's sentences. To use my earlier phrase, they "desecrated upward." They skillfully and thoroughly shifted the tone of the language from the roughness of Tyndale's plowboy to the smooth speech of the royal court. Most of the translators, after all, were part of the "old boy" network of King James, many of them bishops who lived a comfortable and protected life among the elite of the age. Adam Nicolson, author of a thorough study of the King James translators and an extravagant admirer of their work, is also explicit that

> the King James Bible . . . is not the English you would have heard on the street, then or ever. . . . These scholars were not putting the language of the scriptures into the English they knew and used at home. The words of the King James Bible are just as much English pushed towards the condition of a foreign language as a foreign language translated into English. It was, in other words, more important to make English godly than to make the words of God into the sort of prose that any Englishmen would have written. . . . Tyndale had produced a simple and plain man's translation to be slapped in the face of the medieval church and its power-protective elite. . . . [He was] looking for immediacy and clarity in scripture which would shake off the thick and heavy layers of medieval scholasticism and centuries of accumulated dust.[25]

The forty-seven King James translators, working in the sumptuous furnishings of the great universities and the royal court and relying largely on Tyndale's work (work he had done single-handed as a

---

24. Actual computer-based statistics are 83 percent for the New Testament and 76 percent for the Old Testament. See David Daniell, *The Bible in English: Its History and Influence* (New Haven: Yale University Press, 2003), p. 448.

25. Nicolson, *God's Secretaries*, pp. 211-12.

hunted exile on the run from the King of England eighty-five years before), essentially undid his work, turning his plain speech into the majestic grandeur of the King James Version. Making the English of his
day the language of the Bible, Tyndale translated, "The Lord was with
Joseph and he was a luckie felawe"; the King James translators translated "upward" to "and the LORD was with Joseph, and he was a pros-
perous man" (Gen. 39:2). The King James translators put out a version
of the Bible that became the literary classic of the Western world, but at
the expense of Tyndale's plowboy.

That this is the Bible of choice for so many people, across the
years and today (it is not known if they read it or not), is a great irony.[26]

The Ugarit and Oxyrhynchus discoveries revealed a world of everydayness and a language of everydayness that plunges readers of the Bible
into our own everydayness. Their cumulative effect is to overturn a
huge barricade that interferes with a personal, relational reading of
Scripture, namely, the supposition that it is written in a set-apart language, a religious language that comes out of sacred places and rituals,
a language composed of words that were whispered or spoken in rev-
erential tones.

The surprise at Oxyrhynchus has to do with the language in
which the New Testament was written — not a "Holy Ghost" language
but a common street language that the Holy Spirit uses to "divide soul
from spirit, joints from marrow" (Heb. 4:12 NRSV).[27] Virtually anyone
can read this Bible with understanding if it is translated into the kind of
language in which it was written. We don't have to be smart or well ed-

---

26. The church and world had to wait four hundred years for a translator who
would take up Tyndale's passion for getting the Scriptures into the language of "the
plowboy." James Moffatt, a Scottish pastor and professor, taking his cue from the recently discovered papyri, gave us the first vernacular translation in English since Tyndale (the New Testament in 1913; full Bible in 1926).

27. It is not all street language, to be sure. Hebrews in the New Testament is written in an elegant and polished Greek and Isaiah in the Old Testament is written in a
most exquisite poetry. With plenty of other exceptions — but they are *exceptions* — for
the most part our Scriptures are in the language of the common people.

ucated in order to understand it any more than its first readers did. It is written in the same language we use when we go shopping, play games, or ask for a second helping of potatoes at the supper table — and it requires translation into that same language.

At Ugarit the surprise is culture, the culture in which our Hebrew ancestors, the children of Israel, lived and died. Previous to the discovery of Ugarit, we knew very little of the Canaanite culture in which our Hebrew ancestors lived. Lacking information, it was easy to imagine the Hebrews, the saved people of God, leaving Egypt, disciplined to a life of obedience and holiness in the forty years of wilderness wandering, and then entering Canaan armed and prepared to carve out a holy culture all to themselves. That is not the way it happened. Nor is it the way it is now.

The Oxyrhynchus and Ugarit discoveries have far more to do with the tone of the language than the accuracy of the text, although accuracies are sometimes involved. Their primary effect is to counter this creeping and seemingly innocent sacrilege upward to which all language, but especially biblical language, is vulnerable, and which insidiously removes the biblical text from its rootage in the actual ground on which we live our lives.

If there is anything distinctive about *The Message,* perhaps it is that the text is shaped by the hand of a working pastor. For most of my adult life I have been given a primary responsibility for getting the message of the Bible into the lives of the men and women with whom I worked. I did it from pulpit and lectern, in home Bible studies and at mountain retreats, through conversations in hospitals and nursing homes, over coffee in kitchens and while strolling on an ocean beach. *The Message* grew from the soil of thirty-five years of pastoral work. As I did this work, making choices of words and phrases, I was often aware of how thoroughly I was being influenced by those thirty-five years of pastoral life. I was translating for the saints and sinners who were trying to find their way in the muddle and mess of the world. I identified with the first writers and readers/listeners of Scripture, whose first concern had to do with living in the company of the Trinity while walking down the muddy roads of Galilee and Judea and navigating through the sexual chaos of Corinth. Theology, making coherent sense of God's revelation in our lives, comes later. I was doing my work for those who were aware of the urgency of life here and now — and for God. I was translating "so he may run who reads" (Hab. 2:2).

As I worked at this task, I could see that this word of God that should form and transform human lives did in fact form and transform human lives. Planted in the soil of my congregation and community, the seed words of the Bible germinated and grew and matured. When it came time to do the work that is now *The Message,* I often felt that I was walking through an orchard at harvest time, plucking fully formed apples and peaches and plums from laden branches. There is hardly a page in the Bible that I did not see lived in some way or other by the men and women, saints and sinners, to whom I was pastor, and then, as I looked around, saw verified in my nation and culture. Or, to change the image, when a zeal for Holy Scripture and a zeal for common language collide, sparks fly. Sometimes the sparks become a translation. They did for me.

I didn't start out as a pastor. I began my vocational life as a teacher and for several years taught the biblical languages of Hebrew and Greek in a theological seminary. I expected to live the rest of my life as a professor and scholar, teaching, writing, and studying. But then my life took a sudden vocational turn and I became a pastor in a congregation. My workplace shifted from a classroom of saints and sinners to a congregation of saints and sinners.

I found myself in a very different world. The first noticeable difference was that nobody seemed to care much about the Bible, which so recently people had been paying me to teach them. Many of the people with whom I now worked knew virtually nothing about it — had never read it and weren't interested in learning. Many others had spent years reading it, but for them it had gone flat through familiarity and been reduced to sclerotic clichés. Bored, they dropped it. And there weren't many people in between. Very few of them were interested in what I considered an essential element in my primary work, getting the words of the Bible into their heads and hearts, getting the message lived. They found newspapers, videos, and pulp fiction more to their taste.

Meanwhile, I had taken on as my life work the responsibility of getting these very people to listen, really listen, to the message in this book. I knew I had my work cut out for me.

I started out by explaining the Bible to my congregation, getting them to buy study books — dictionaries and concordances to start with. There was so much to know! And I had so much to tell them!

In the midst of doing this, it occurred to me that the first people who heard or read the Bible didn't need a dictionary or a concordance. When Isaiah preached, the people didn't have to organize a seminar and hire a professor to figure out what he said. When Mark's Gospel showed up in a community, they didn't feel the necessity of putting together a six-month study course on Wednesday evenings. All these books came out of the common life and common knowledge of the people, many, maybe even most, of them illiterate. Not unintelligent, mind you, but not schooled. So why was I intruding all my knowledge *about* the Bible into their reading of it?

So I shifted my style of teaching. Instead of informing them of Ugaritic words that illuminated the Hebrew text, instead of working through the intricacies of the synoptic variations in the stories and words of Jesus, instead of testing Paul's language against the Hellenistic philosophies and mystery cults, I just gathered people together to *read* the text as we have it. Their first response was almost always, "We can't understand this; tell us what it means — you're the one who has been to seminary." But I persisted. Together we would just read it imaginatively and prayerfully, try to enter into the words on the page as they were before us. Sometimes I would ask questions, hinting and guiding a little to observe what was there, giving them confidence to go ahead and bring the same kind of reading to the biblical text that they used in reading the morning newspaper. Most of the time, after an hour or so with a page of text, they would have come up with virtually everything of substance that could also be found in the commentaries. I was not averse to bringing in tidbits of lexical or archaeological lore that spiced things up. But mostly I trusted them to read the text.

There is a fancy word for what became clear in these gatherings: *perspicuity* — the conviction that the Bible is basically readable as it is. It is not a body of secret lore accessible only to an academic elite. It is written plainly for plain men and women.

I lived in two language worlds, the world of the Bible and the world of today. I had always assumed that they were the same world, but these people didn't see it that way. So out of necessity I became a translator, daily standing between the two worlds, helping them hear the language of the Bible that God uses to create and save us, heal and bless us, judge and rule over us in the language of today that we use to gossip and tell stories, give directions and do business, sing songs and talk to our children.

And all the time those old biblical languages, those powerful and vivid Hebrew and Greek originals, were working their way underground in my speech, giving sharpness and energy to words and phrases, expanding the imagination of the people with whom I was working in the language of today — the language of today mined from the language of the Bible.

Lost in Translation

My wife and I were lost in Jerusalem one day. It was a day that I had decided to speak only in Hebrew. My Hebrew is all book Hebrew, classroom Hebrew, Bible Hebrew. I had never before encountered Hebrew as a living language. We had been in Israel for a couple of weeks and I woke up that morning realizing that now I had my chance. I wanted to see if I could make my way through just a single day using only this language that was so important to me. By now it was late in the evening in Jerusalem and my wife and I were lost. We were looking for a restaurant that had been recommended to us. We had the address but couldn't find it. We were hopelessly disoriented. We met a couple walking toward us who seemed likely to be Jewish. In my halting, clumsy Hebrew I asked for help — apologizing for bothering them but hoping they could get us at least pointed in the right direction. They listened patiently and courteously. When I had finished they broke into wide grins, "We're from Detroit!" And then they gave us the directions we needed — but in English. After sampling my spoken Hebrew, they clearly did not trust me to hear their Hebrew well enough to get us to the restaurant.

"We're from Detroit" is language used naturally and spontaneously, but hardly literally. Too much is lost in translation when it is done literally. The couple could have answered me literally, using the Hebrew in which they were fluent. And if they had been willing to speak very slowly and repeat themselves enough times, I would have gotten the help I had asked for. But we got much more. Their "we're from Detroit" put language to use at a very different level: it conveyed welcome, delight in being able to help us, a total absence of condescension regarding my awkward and inadequate Hebrew. We got more than directions to the restaurant; we were given a gift, however brief, of friendship. This man and woman were not content to use language reduced to a mere exchange of information. They did not ignore our need for directions but they also revealed something of themselves, their common humanity with us, their incipient hospitality.

"We're from Detroit" gives me a benchmark from which to reflect on the way translation works. To begin with, translation is not only between languages, it is implicit wherever and whenever language is used. It is not restricted to what happens when we translate, say, German into English. There is plenty of translation that takes place everyday in getting the American English I speak into the American English that you hear. I did it every Sunday from a pulpit and every day while raising my children, and I soon learned that I could take nothing for granted. We all use words differently. And we misunderstand frequently. Language is ambiguous. We have to repeat often and explain patiently. As we listen and respond to the speech of those around us, parents and children, teachers and students, government leaders and citizens, pastors and congregations, coaches and players, husbands and wives, we are constantly "translating," using everything we can get our hands on to get it right: body language, tone of voice, our history with this other person, the present circumstances in which we are placed, and also, of course, but never in isolation, the dictionary meaning of the words and the grammatical structure of the sentences.

The complexity involved in all of this forces the realization that a literal translation, apart from translating scientific data and information transfer, is almost always inadequate. And why? Because a literal translation excludes all the nonverbal dimensions that are at work whenever language is used. It also mindlessly repeats idioms, metaphors, and sentence structures that have no context in the receiving language.

Translation is a complex activity that takes place between a polarity of two questions. The question asked from one pole is, "What did he say?" The question from the other pole is, "What did she mean?"

"What did he say?" answered strictly on its own terms yields a literal translation. Find the German word equivalent to the English word and that's it. A dictionary and grammar, a familiarity with the literature and culture of the language to be translated, are required.

"What did she mean?" requires an imagination, often a poetic imagination, that brings the "world" of the German text into the "world" of American English, and this necessarily involves a re-creation of the text into another language. Far more is required than a dictionary and grammar in order to translate. We need a familiarity with the "life" that is being translated; but we also require a familiarity with the "life" into which it is being translated. Sebastian Brock champions the primacy of "What did she mean?" in translation: "In the case of free translation, it could be said that the original is brought to the reader, but with the literal type the reader is forced to go to the original; or, to put it another way, in the first it is the reader who is stationary, but in the second it is the original."[28] Each language is an intricate and living culture, a culture distilled in words, spread out in language. If all we are translating is dictionary meanings, the entire culture is lost

28. Sebastian Brock, "The Phenomenon of Biblical Translation in Antiquity," in *Studies in the Septuagint: Origins, Recensions, and Interpretations,* ed. Sidney Jellicoe (New York: KTAV, 1974).

in translation. Henry Wadsworth Longfellow, one of the great American poets in the nineteenth century and professor of languages at Yale University, translated Dante's *Divine Comedy* into English. One of his critics complained that he had translated the *Comedy* into the English dictionary, not the English language.[29] And it is the culture — the way of living and thinking, believing and behaving, the assumptions and allusions — that requires translation as far as we are able. Like, "we're from Detroit."

In my work as pastor and writer, teacher and preacher, I began to gather observations and witnesses on the nature of translation, noticing how unsatisfactory "literal" turns out to be and how conveniently it serves as cover for avoiding the obvious intent of words spoken or written. But it is as parent and grandparent that most of us accumulate the most telling evidence.

One evening our family was gathered around the supper table. The grandchildren had been excused to leave the table and play. A few minutes later, Hans, seven years old, came at full gallop through the dining room followed by his two little sisters. His father said, "Hans, there is no running in the house." Hans shortened his stride by about eight inches and said, "I'm not running; I'm jogging" — a case study in literalism, common among children, as a way of avoiding meaning. But adults are not exempt.

An old canard that sooner or later gets introduced into discussions of translation is, "You, a translator? You're a traitor!" (In Italian, *Traduttore? traditore!*) Translation is betrayal. All translation is inherently mistranslation. Each language is unique. The particular genius of a language cannot be carried over into another. By this criterion every translation is an adulteration of the original, a watering down, a reduction. And if the language being translated is the word of God, and translation by its very nature is falsification, then we'd better not do it.

Oh?

29. John Ahern, "Vulgar Eloquence," *NY Times Review of Books* (January 1, 1995).

This position was actually espoused during the time when the King James Bible was being translated. John Smyth was a pastor of the Brethren of the Separation of the Second English Church at Amsterdam in 1608, a congregation made up of Lincolnshire farmers, Puritans in exile from English persecution. Smyth and his congregation held that every translation, however good, was bound to contain errors and so by definition could not be used. They needed to hear the Scriptures in the original. If God had spoken in Hebrew, Greek, and Aramaic, those were the languages in which he should be heard. And so hour after hour in their meetings, Smyth read out the Scripture passages of Hebrew and Aramaic and Greek, of which his congregation had not the faintest understanding.[30]

Such a stubborn insistence on the "literal original" is, of course, a parody of what is modified by good sense among most of the rest of us. But "literal" continues to represent in the minds of many the ideal in matters of translation.

Preference for the literal has a long life. But I have come to believe that it is an unthinking preference. My experience as a parent supplemented by my experience as a pastor cautions me that the peril of the literal is that it ignores the inherent ambiguities in all language, takes the source language prisoner and force-marches it, shackled and chained, into an English that nobody living speaks. The language is lobotomized — the very quality that gives language its genius, its capacity to reveal what we otherwise would not know, is excised. Extreme literalism insists on forcing each word into a fixed immovable position, all the sentences strapped into a straitjacket. I began to see why Luther, the grandfather of Reformation translators, did not take kindly to the critics who bashed his vernacular translation. He called them "those lemmings the literalists."[31]

In recent years William Griffin has taken to translating a number of Christianity's Latin classics into English. He writes that when he set out on this task,

<hr />

30. See Nicolson, *God's Secretaries*, p. 181.
31. Nicolson, *God's Secretaries*, p. 195.

I fully intended to do the literal translation, of course, and yes, better than any of my predecessors had done, but I soon found myself faltering. Fidelity seemed its only virtue. Felicity was nowhere to be seen. But Fidelity without Felicity in translation can be a very mean virtue indeed. . . . As many before me, I'd always thought Paraphrase was bonkers. Why? Because my intellectual betters had told me so, and I had no occasion to say them nay. But what they never told me in so many words was that all translation was all too errant. Soon thereafter I concluded that if err I must, then I'd prefer to err on the side of Paraphrase rather than Literalese.[32]

Griffin goes on to provide a most entertaining but seriously instructive apology for paraphrase, which, if doesn't eliminate, at least tempers the condescension to which it is commonly treated by those of a literalist bent.

The African theologian Kwame Bediako further loosens the grip of literalese on our presuppositions by showing how translation in the African context, instead of taking responsibility for preserving the unique particularities of the biblical Hebrew and Greek, takes delight in releasing it in a new and fresh form. George Steiner, who writes with more insight and learning on translation than anyone I know, affirms the soundness of Bediako's position when he insists that translation gives "the original a new resonance, a longer life, a wider readership, a more substantial place in history and culture."[33] Writing out of the context of the many African languages into which Scripture has been translated, Bediako notes that each of these African mother tongues has its own unique syntax and character, and so its own way of making its contribution to a fuller hearing of the inexhaustible riches of the word of God. Rather than diluting the pure word of God, each new translation elaborates it, provides fresh settings or contexts, offers

32. William Griffin, "In Praise of Paraphrase," *Books and Culture* 8, no. 5 (Sept.-Oct. 2002).

33. George Steiner, *Errata: An Examined Life* (New Haven: Yale University Press, 1997), p. 112.

metaphors that provide yet another access to transcendence; each translation creates refractions of the "immortal, invisible, God only wise" in words that add to the store of insight and adoration that provides us with fresh annunciations of the gospel in our common lives as the communion of saints worldwide. Bediako notes that the ease and frequency with which the Christian Scriptures have been translated into so many "mother tongues" can be accounted for by the refusal of the original biblical writers to use a "sacred" language. Christianity in the course of its expansion developed generally as a "vernacular religion." He uses the African experience as documentation: "how fully at home we Africans have become in the Gospel of Jesus Christ. Each one of us, with access to the Bible in our mother-tongue, can truly claim to hear God speaking to us in our own language!"[34] Jacques Derrida from a very different perspective supports Bediako's position when he writes that "the translation will truly be a moment in the growth of the original, which will complete itself *in* enlarging itself." He refers to translation as a marriage contract with the promise "to produce a child whose seed will give rise to history and growth."[35]

Translation is interpretation. Always. It is interpretation because words always convey far more meaning than the dictionary assigns them. Words have histories, emotional associations, story-influenced connotations. And interpretation requires — to one degree or another — paraphrase.

My first experience with biblical paraphrase was J. B. Phillips's *Letters to Young Churches,* a translation in paraphrase of the New Testament Epistles. I got my copy in 1948, a year after it had been published in England. I was a high school student. At the time I was a faithful and diligent Bible reader, but by means of Phillips's paraphrase, my Bible reading became personal at a depth that it had never been before. My

34. Kwame Bediako, *Jesus in African Culture: A Ghanaian Perspective* (Accra: Presbyterian Press, 1990), pp. 43-44.

35. Quoted in Joseph F. Graham, ed., *Difference in Translation* (Ithaca: Cornell University Press, 1985), pp. 188-202.

only Bible until then was the King James Version in the Scofield Reference Edition. It not only gave me the biblical text in majestically sonorous English but supplied me with extensive footnotes that instructed me in how to interpret what I was reading. I read the notes with as much or more care as I did the text. I *studied* the Scofield King James on the hunt for inspiration or gathering data for bull-session arguments to refute or convert my friends. When I read devotionally, I read mindlessly, taking in the inspired words with about the same degree of participation with which I received an IV the time I was in the hospital to get my appendix removed, the medicine needled directly into my vein, bypassing the brain. Most of what I have later come to appreciate and honor as the word of God as it has formed my life — the quotidian tone, the all-encompassing story, the earthy poetry, the personal and prayerful participation — was lost in translation.

But Phillips gave me a Bible I could *read* — and I read and read and read. He introduced me to the world of Scripture, not just its words; he immersed me in its marvelous sentences, helped me to feel the impact of the metaphors. In describing his experience of translating, he wrote that he often "felt like an electrician re-wiring an ancient house, without being able to 'turn the mains off.'"[36] I later learned that the first readers of his translation were young people of my age in the youth group in the London parish where Phillips was pastor. Translation was a pastoral act, his attempt to get the language of the Bible into the language world of his London adolescents. It wasn't long before it made its way across the ocean and all the way west to Montana into the language world in which I and my friends lived. As he continued in the years following to translate the rest of the New Testament and a first installment of the Old, I avidly bought each new volume. Each edition expanded and deepened my sense of and participation in what "biblical" was — an immediate world to live in, not a remote world to decipher and figure out.

I kept reading. In a few years I was reading the Bible in Hebrew

36. J. B. Phillips, *Letters to Young Churches: A Translation of the New Testament Epistles* (New York: Macmillan, 1953), p. ix.

and Greek and finding that the first-handedness, the at-homeness that Phillips had invited me into, was confirmed in the style and tone in which these Scriptures were first written and read, and that the only way that style and tone could be conveyed to the people among whom I lived was through paraphrase. Thanks to this pastor-translator, the biblical text carried me out of the small, cramped world of "figuring out" the text into the large, immense world of God's revelation witnessed by the text. "Biblical" for me came to mean living, imagining, believing, loving, conversing in this world, living in this precisely rendered and richly organic context which comes to full expression in Jesus (who talked in street language) and to which I was given access by the Old and New Testaments of the Bible. It did not mean cobbling texts together to prove or substantiate a dogma or a practice. "Biblical" no longer meant merely referring to the Bible or substantiating my position from the Bible. It referred to a world — "the strange new world within the Bible" (Barth) — a world in which most of what takes place is invisible but with visible effects, a world in which I was a full participant — *involved.*

In retrospect, I realize that Phillips not only invited me into and made me at home in the world of God's revelation by means of his translation, he showed me how to do it, sowed the seeds that sixty years later would be harvested as *The Message.*

What was done for me, I found myself wanting to do for others, doing everything I could to show men and women that the Scriptures are *livable* — that God's word is personal address, inviting, commanding, challenging, rebuking, judging, comforting, directing — but not forcing. Not coercing. We are given space and freedom in these biblical pages to answer, to enter into the conversation. More than anything else the Bible invites our participation in the work and language of God.

I wanted to help my friends see the organic connection between the word read and the word lived. I wanted to get the street language of Jerusalem — "we're from Detroit!" — onto American streets. I wanted to convey by means of American syntax and diction that everything in this book is livable, that the most important question is not "What does it say?" but "What does it mean and how can I live it?" I wanted to gather a company of people together who read personally, not impersonally, who learned to read the Bible in order to live their true selves, not just get information that they could use to raise their standard of living. I wanted to counter the consumer attitude that uses the Bible as a way to gather religious data by which we can be our own gods, and then replace it with an attitude primed to listen to and obey God, to take us out of our preoccupations with ourselves into the spacious freedom in which God is working the world's salvation. I wanted to somehow recover that original tone, that prophetic and gospel "voice" that stabs us awake to a beauty and hope that connects us with our real lives.

I wanted this first for myself, then for my congregation and all who read and listen to *The Message*. But I am also aware that I'm not alone in this. Many, very many, men and women have preceded me in this work. And many more will continue the work. Translation takes place on multi-levels: study Bibles, reference Bibles, revisions of early translations, translations more suitable for formal worship, translations working along a spectrum of language from formal to colloquial. All, or at least most, are useful to the reading and worshipping Christian community. *The Message* comes out of a specific setting and time in our American culture and is not meant to replace but rather to supplement the excellent translations presently available. I am very conscious that I am in a vast company of translators — teachers in classrooms, pastors in pulpits, parents around the supper table, writers in languages all over the world, baptized Christians in workplaces and social gatherings past imagining — all of us at this same work, collaborators in translating the word of God, reading and then living this text, eating the book, and then getting these Scriptures into whatever language is heard and spoken on the street on which we live.

Some Writers on Spiritual Reading

The ease with which most of us read masks the enormous difficulty involved in reading. It is customary among us to acquire the rudiments of reading in the first three or four years of our schooling. Society insists that we know how to read. An army of teachers is recruited and maintained, schools are constructed and classrooms furnished to make sure that all of us learn to read from an early age. Reading is not only necessary for our own good; it is necessary for the good of our nation. Our parents and our government agree, at least, in this. And so adequate reading skills are routinely taught so that we are prepared to function as responsible citizens. Most of us can read the newspapers, instruction manuals, street signs, comic strips, the latest novel, love letters, invoices, computer screens, and get on quite well in the world, thank you.

But despite the money and time our society expends in teaching us to read, nobody gives much attention or energy to teaching *how* to read. Among our ancestors reading involved a seeking after wisdom, becoming a mature person. With us it is more likely to be a retrieval of information so that we can answer a question or do a job. Spiritual reading is not contemptuous of information, but it has wisdom for its goal: *becoming* true and good, not just knowing about the facts of life or how to change a tire.

In our information-gluttonous world, spiritual reading is hardly mentioned. I find that I need considerable help frequently provided to prevent my being swept away and suffocated in the avalanche of words that have been reduced to their informational or functional dimensions. Here are seven writers that have proved reliable and sturdy companions as I read both books and *the* book.

Karl Barth, *Church Dogmatics,* vol. 1: *The Doctrine of the Word of God,* part 1.

Christians read Scripture not as just another book off the shelf in the library but as, precisely, revelation — God revealing himself to us. This requires a wholesale rethinking and re-imagining of the way we read. How does it happen that the same words that we use in our everyday speech with one another can also be used as words that reveal God to us? How does it happen that, in Barth's fine phrase, "The Lord of speech is also the Lord of our hearing of it" — God as active in our reading of the revelation as in the prophets' and apostles' writing of it? This is a large book (560 pages), but for me, at least, it takes a long time, accompanied by many repetitions and re-readings, to exchange my practical, Americanized training in how to read a book for something adequate for taking in the word of God. (Edinburgh: T. & T. Clark, 1936)

Ivan Illich, *In the Vineyard of the Text.*

Hugh of St. Victor, one of our seminal figures in the field of spiritual theology, in about A.D. 1150 wrote the first book on the art of spiritual reading (the *Didascalion*), treating it as an intricate and comprehensive ascetic discipline. Ivan Illich's commentary on the book provides us access to this incomparable trove of insights, counsel, and urgency embedded in the practice of spiritual reading. (Chicago: University of Chicago Press, 1996)

Austin Farrer, *The Glass of Vision.*

Christians read the revelation of God that is written in our Holy Scriptures because we believe that in some way or other it is inspired by the Holy Spirit. Our Bible does not merely convey information about God but, if received rightly, *is* God's word supernaturally at work in us. But what precisely does that mean? How does that happen? There is no scarcity of theories on inspiration. Farrer probes the *how* with more imagination than most, providing images that include us as participants in the inspiration, not as men and women who just talk about it or assent to it. (Westminster: Dacre, 1948)

Northrop Frye, *The Great Code: The Bible and Literature.*

The *way* the Bible is written — the way words are used, sentences are formed, poetry fashioned — is as much a part of the text as *what* is written. That is, the Bible is not truth in the abstract. The doctrine of the Trinity, the incarnation of the word in Jesus, and the life of David are written in distinctive ways, using language that is full of nuance and beauty, surprise and austerity, using language across the full range of testimony and imagination involved in this witness to the revelation of God. If all we are after is the theological ideas and salvation facts, we miss the richness and complexity that is involved on every page of Scripture. Northrop Frye is an incomparable teacher in all matters having to do with the language of the Bible, deepening both our understanding and our appreciation of the way it is written "for us and for our salvation." (New York: Harcourt Brace Jovanovich, 1982)

Paul Ricoeur, *Essays on Biblical Interpretation.*

The moment we set out to read and pray, teach and preach, understand and live Holy Scripture we find ourselves immersed in thoroughly uncongenial conditions. Our vaunted communication technologies systematically depersonalize and reduce language, which is to say, relentlessly empty the spirit from the letter. It is one of the most striking features of our age. How do we recover the living quality of language, restore our sensitivity to its original nature as precisely *revelatory* — soul-revealing, God-revealing? Paul Ricoeur for many of us has been our premier teacher in this arduous work of interpreting the text (the discipline of "hermeneutics") against the corrosively secularizing spirit of the times. (Edited by Lewis S. Mudge. Philadelphia: Fortress, 1980)

George Steiner, *Real Presences.*

We live in a ruthlessly secularizing age in which language is flattened into a thin, one-dimensional sheet of tin, all transcendence squeezed out. Words are "just" words, puffs of air, incapable of conveying spirit or presence, let alone God. If the age is correct about this, nothing that we read, including the Bible, conveys meaning much beyond the ink on the page. Steiner vigorously argues the reverse, that meaning is inherent in all language, that language is underwritten by the assumption of God's presence. The implications for the ways in which we listen and read are enormous. The recovery and practice of *spiritual* reading is urgent across the board but nowhere more so than in our reading of the Scriptures. (Chicago: University of Chicago Press, 1989)

C. S. Lewis, *An Experiment in Criticism*

Lewis's last book, published near the end of his life, is a fitting last word from the man who taught so many of my generation to read imaginatively, accurately, and devoutly. Virtually any book, whether Lewis wrote it or read it, was for him a way into reality, both human-reality and God-reality. Intelligence distilled into wisdom, accumulated over a lifetime of reading, is his final legacy to us. (Cambridge: Cambridge University Press, 1992, Canto edition; first published in 1961)

Index of Subjects and Names

Index of Scripture References

Also in this series:

Christ Plays in Ten Thousand Places
A Conversation in Spiritual Theology

Eugene H. Peterson

*This is a book for all places, for all times and for all situations,
however tragic and hopeless they may seem to be.*
Gehard Hughes

Christ Plays in Ten Thousand Places is the first volume in the
series of five, and concentrates on establishing the landscape
within which Peterson's exploration unfolds.

Most writings in the field of spiritual theology represent mere
dabblings. The more significant endeavours are impenetrably
academic. Peterson's masterwork, which has been years in the
making, is designed for those who are comfortable with being
stretched, as well as pastors, academics and lay leaders.

The best-selling author of *The Message* draws on the very
latest scholarship and understanding of biblical revelation,
and represents the most thorough and significant work on
contemporary Christian Spirituality by an evangelical author.

ISBN 0340 863889

Hodder & Stoughton
www.madaboutbooks.co.uk
and
www.hodderbibles.co.uk

The Spiritual Formation Bible
Combines the depth of a study bible with the heart of a devotional bible

Editors:
Richard Foster, Dallas Willard, Walter Brueggemann,
Eugene Peterson

If the pressures of work, family or ministry allow you time to read only one book this year, The Spiritual Formation Bible *would be an excellent choice. It is unrivalled as a classic work of biblical theology suffused with a pastoral heart.*
Brennan Manning

At last – a truly twenty-first century Study Bible. In this major new Bible, the foremost names in Christian spirituality and biblical scholarship have combined to produce a unique Bible that rediscovers Scripture as living text.

The book includes
- The full text of the NRSV Bible
- Introductions and notes for each book of the Bible
- Spiritual exercises incorporated throughout the text
- Profiles of key biblical characters
- 15 essays on living 'The With-God Life'
- Spiritual Disciplines Index – a glossary and complete Bible references for all the spiritual disciplines

ISBN 0340 909013

Hodder & Stoughton

www.madaboutbooks.co.uk
and
www.hodderbibles.co.uk

NIV/The Message Parallel Bible

Make the connection between your every day life and God's Word.

The NIV – today's most popular and trusted modern translation of the Bible is teamed with *The Message* – Eugene Peterson's easy-to-read, contemporary Scripture translation – to bring the Bible to life. The clean, easy-to-use juxtaposition of Bible passage and paraphrase allows deeper understanding of Scripture and will encourage new perceptions of the text for readers of all ages and denominations.

This edition contains the full text of both *The Message* and the NIV.

ISBN 0340 863862

TNIV/The Message Remix Bible

TNIV paired with the popular Remix edition of The Message.

TNIV is a thoroughly accurate, fully trustworthy Bible text built on the rich heritage of the NIV. It presents the fruit of the ongoing study of the same team of translators that were responsible for the original NIV. The uniqueness of TNIV rests on its ability to speak God's word clearly and accurately in English that has developed and changed over the last quarter century. The result is a Bible text that reflects the NIV, but also clarifies and updates passages and words to provide a more timely, contemporary English rendition for a new generation of Bible readers.

The Message Remix is a fast-growing, popular 'reader's Bible'. Set in a clean, easy-to-read parallel design, it is the perfect combination for readers who enjoy viewing the scriptures from a variety of angles.

ISBN 0340 908955

Hodder & Stoughton
www.hodderbibles.co.uk